ARMS AND ARMOUR
TRADITIONAL WEAPONS OF INDIA

E. JAIWANT PAUL

India Crest

Lustre Press
Roli Books

DEDICATION

for Shubh

Previous pages (LEFT TO RIGHT)
Jade hilt set with precious stones, Mughal (Delhi), Early 17th century A.D.; Katar (jamdhar) blade carved with hunting scenes, Rajasthan; Talwar pommel and knuckle guard composed of animal forms, with a perforated and embellished scabbard, Rajasthan, 17th century A.D.; Spearhead; Mace with damascened flanges and spikes on the head, North India, 18th century A.D.; Katar (jamdhar) blade with thickened point.

CONTENTS

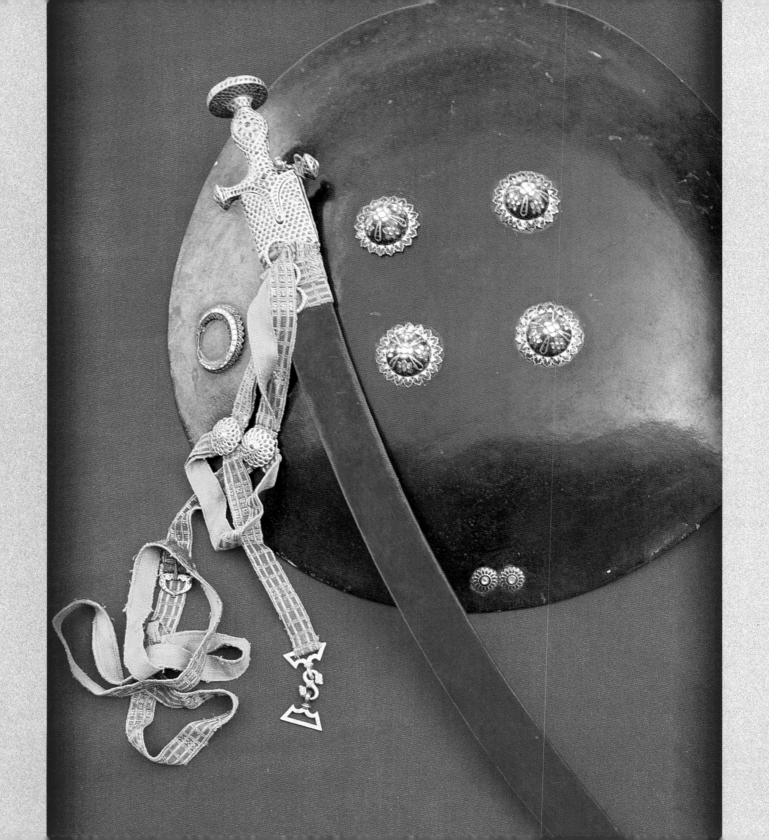

INTRODUCTION

Traditionally man has had a deep, almost instinctive, reverence and love for his weapons. He holds them sacred and invests them with a sort of divine power. He treasures and preserves them, and armourers embellish them with priceless gems, gold and silver. In some countries arms were laid in graves with their masters and weapons of war were sacrificially deposited in hallowed spots. Even today the Rajputs and Marathas, the two races who through history have risen to defend the honour of this country, bring out their weapons on the festival of Dussehra and worship them in an elaborate ritual. Stressing the great value placed on arms, it was once observed, *what greater thing can a king own than the armour which protects his body during combat*? The reasons for this instinctive veneration and esteem are varied. Man may feel a deep attachment towards a weapon which has saved his life and which accompanies and protects him. Arms also signify the risking of one's life for the protection of one's country, ideals, culture and honour. But other than these, arms are also a test of courage and a demonstration of strength, manhood, pride, virtue, victory, justice and freedom.

Arms may also signify the ultimate and supreme sacrifice as well as the involvement of life with death. This twin involvement of arms with life and death is symbolized by kings of yore going into battle in magnificent array, clad in beauteous armour and marked by the royal *chattri* or umbrella, knowing full well that their glittering

Facing page

❖ **SHIELD AND SWORD.** *The shield made of rhinoceros hide is lacquered in black. The sword has an embellished standard Indian hilt. The straps called 'kamarsal or bandtar' are elaborate. They either fasten around the waist or are hung over the shoulder.*

attire could just as easily be transformed into a shroud. But this panoply, this exuberance was an essential element not only in the celebration of life but also in man's defiance of death.

Weapons have always intrigued mankind, because mankind has always been intrigued by war. Centuries ago it was said:

> War is a joyous thing. You love your comrades so and when you know your quarrel is just and your blood is fighting well, tears rise to your eyes and out of that arises such pleasure and delight. Can anyone who has tasted that pleasure fear death?

The aesthetic appreciation of a well made weapon is greatly amplified by holding it and when possible, by using it. The sword firmly held in the hand becomes an extension of the arm. It becomes one with the body. You feel its strength and authority for the sword has the power of life and death.

In his *Annals and Antiquities of Rajasthan*, first published in 1829, Col. James Tod describes the *karga shapna* or the worship of the sword. In Mewar, this rite is performed during the Navratri festival, when the Mother Goddess is worshipped over a period of

nine days. The weapon worshipped was the *khanda*, the Rajput straight sword.

On the first day the *khanda* is removed from the hall of arms *(awadsala)*, and having received the homage of the court, is carried in a procession to the Kishenpol (gate of Kishen). Here it is delivered to the *raj jogi* at the temple of Devi, the goddess of battle, and is placed on the altar. The *nakaras* or grand kettledrums, about 8 to 10 feet in diameter, signal from the *tripol*, the assemblage of the chiefs and their retainers, for the Rana and his cavalcade to proceed directly to the spot where a buffalo is sacrificed in honour of the war horse. Thence the procession moves to the temple of Devi where the Rana seats himself next to the *raj jogi* and presents him two pieces of silver and a coconut, performs homage to the sword and returns to the palace.

On the fourth day a buffalo is sacrificed by the Rana's own hand. The narrative goes on to say that on the ninth day, at three in the afternoon, the *nakaras* having sounded thrice, the whole state insignia, under a select band, bring home the sword. When its arrival is announced the Rana advances and receives it with all due homage from the hands of the *raj jogi*, who is presented with a *khelat*. The elephants

❖ **HORSE ARMOUR**
Seen here in detail is horse armour made of small, square iron plates interlinked with chain mail—each plate is embellished with a round disc. The armour is flexible and covers the body of the horse.

Facing page

❖ **INSCRIBED DAGGER BLADE (KHANJAR); MUGHAL, LATE 17TH CENTURY, NATIONAL MUSEUM.**

and horses again receive homage and the sword, the shield and the spear are worshipped within the palace.

The tenth day is Dussehra, which is deemed by the Rajputs to be fortunate for warlike enterprises. The day commences with a visit from the prince or chieftain to his spiritual guide. Tents and carpets are prepared at the *choughan* (polo ground) where the artillery is sent; in the afternoon, the Rana, his chiefs and their relatives repair to the 'field of mars' with all the state insignia, the *nakaras* sounding in the rear while the Rana takes muster of his troops amidst discharges of cannon, tilting and displays of horsemanship.

It is worth mentioning that the worship of the sword *(asi)* and the horse *(aswa)* have given the name to the continent of Asia.

The most powerful oath of the Rajput, is by his sovereign's throne *(gadi ki an)* or by his arms *(ya sil ki an)* as suiting the action to the word, he puts his hand on his dagger, never absent from his girdle: *dhal, talwar ki an* (by my sword and shield). The shield is deemed the only fit salver on which to present gifts, and accordingly, at a Rajput court shawls, brocades, scarves and jewels are always spread before the guest on bucklers or shields.

In Rajasthan today, Rajputs form a minority and there are several other races living side by side, including a large proportion of tribals like the Bhils. The Rajput nobility has been in sad decline for over a century and is only a feeble shadow of its ancestors. However, in sharp contrast, their spirit and robustness is very much alive in the Rajput farmers, who are a major asset to the army and join in large numbers.

Interestingly and at the same time surprisingly, swords and daggers from India present a diversity and a range probably unparalleled anywhere in the world. In comparison, European swords are far more conservative. India is a heterogenous country and these variations in the shape, form and style of the Indian sword have evolved over centuries and are the outcome of the martial, cultural and historical traditions of the regions to which they belong.

However, it must be conceded that the dating of weapons is a problematic area. One can judge the age of the weapon by the form and quality of the blade as well as the style of decoration. For instance, on good quality pieces of the sixteenth century the pattern of embellishment is clear and restrained, while later styles tend to become fussy and cover more of the weapon. But

❖ THE ARMS OF A WARRIOR
Katar fitted with two flint lock pistols on the arms of the hilts.

Rajasthani Khanda (1680 A.D.) with a Hindu basket hilt surmounted by a spike. The blade is reinforced with fretted strips.

Metal shield with a turned up rim and decoration.

Helmet with chain mail camail.

Arm guard or bazuband with chain mail gauntlet.

Bhuj fitted with a pistol.

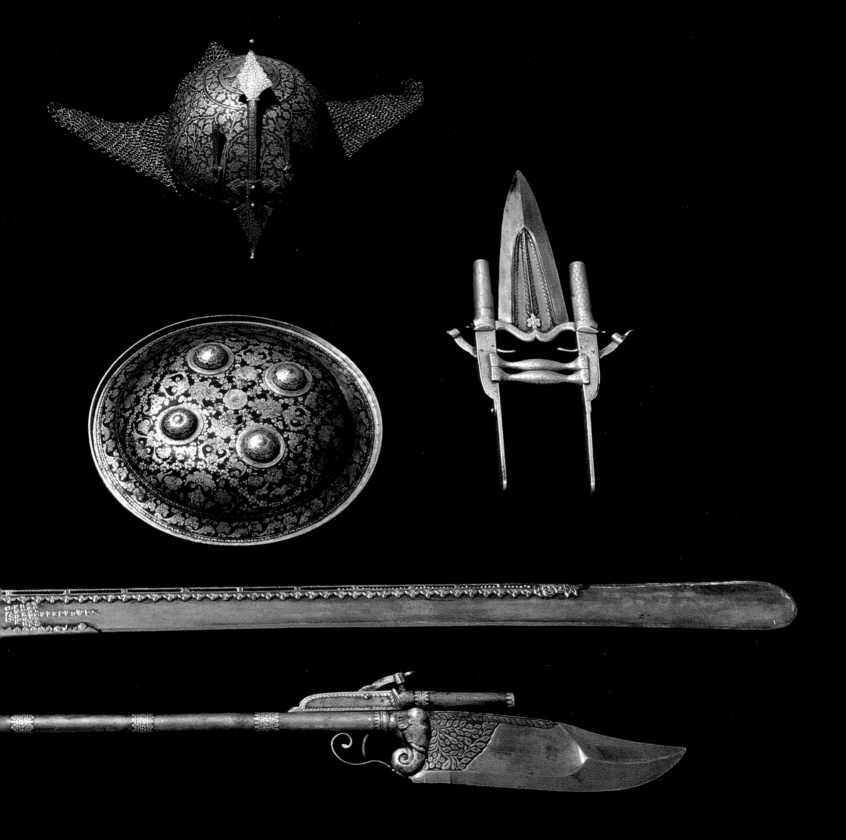

dating can be erroneous because styles and fashions were copied at later times in some regions of the country when they had been abandoned in others. Many swords continued in use long after a new style had been introduced, and many remained in production. All this suggests that dating of weapons must be general rather than specific.

BASIC TERMINOLOGY
~

Before proceeding, it is necessary to get the basic terminology right. There are no standard terms or names for describing the different parts of the hilt or the blade. Many different names have come into use and there is some confusion. The terms in this book are the ones most commonly used and, as far as possible, descriptive ones. The two main parts of the sword and the dagger are the hilt and blade.

The hilt is called *mootha* in Hindi and *quabzah* in Urdu. In the tang button in the hilt, a hole is sometimes made to pass through a safety loop of leather or silk. This sword knot is wrapped round the wrist so that the sword cannot slip out, even if one loses grip.

The blade has two main parts:

the tang that fits into the hilt and the blade proper. The tang is fixed to the hilt with a heated paste of lac or red dye from the peepul tree, which then sets and holds the tang firmly in the hilt.

Sheaths of swords and daggers were usually made of wood covered with velvet, silk or leather. Metal sheaths were also in use and varied from brass to silver and gold. Metal sheaths, however, tended to blunt the sword edge when drawn. Normally, the sheath or scabbard is wide enough to fit the blade but if the blade is sharply curved it is necessary to have a slit in the sheath to accommodate the curve, and the slit is then covered with a flap that buttons down.

An upper fitting is fixed to the top of the sheath and a cap or chape is fixed to the tip of the sheath. A middle fitting was also sometimes used. These fittings are generally embellished lavishly in the same way as the hilt.

Even though cutting and thrusting are both fundamental attributes of the sword, it is necessary to distinguish between swords which are meant primarily for cutting and slashing and those which are used chiefly as thrusting and stabbing weapons. Swords meant solely for thrusting have straight blades, with the length of the blade, its stiffness or rigidity, and the

Parts of the Hilt

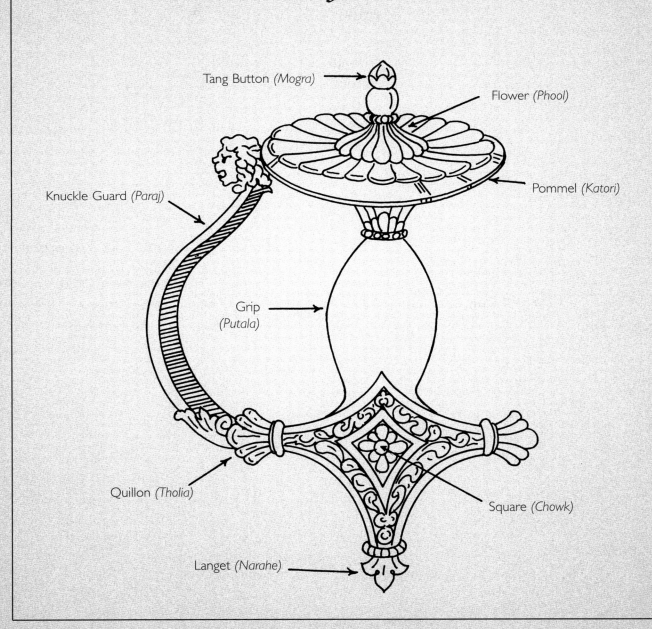

Tang Button *(Mogra)*

Flower *(Phool)*

Knuckle Guard *(Paraj)*

Pommel *(Katori)*

Grip *(Putala)*

Quillon *(Tholia)*

Square *(Chowk)*

Langet *(Narahe)*

Parts of the Blade

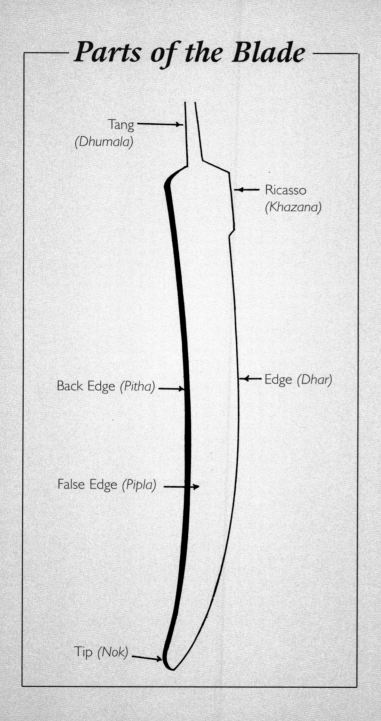

Tang
(Dhumala)

Ricasso
(Khazana)

Back Edge (Pitha)

Edge (Dhar)

False Edge (Pipla)

Tip (Nok)

point or *nok* all assuming greater significance. However, straight swords can also be designed for cutting. The *khanda* and the *dhup* have straight blades, but these are intended for both thrusting and cutting; those with points more suitable for thrusting and those without points for cutting.

On the other hand, swords intended for cutting or slashing have curved blades instead, and this is the main distinction between the two types of swords. Cutting swords are usually single-edged but may have a false edge. The *talwar*, which is an Indian sword, and the *shamsheer*, which had its origins in Persia, both have curved blades and are splendid cutting weapons.

Swords with less curvature in the blade represent a compromise, or the third option, and can be used for both cutting and thrusting, but are not as efficient as those created for a single purpose.

The sword with the backward curve and single edge was an Indo-Persian development. The curved blade achieved a very definite objective—gaining maximum cutting power, sometimes at the expense of other qualities. However, it was ideal for its purpose and could not be improved upon. At the same time it must be appreciated that with the curved blade the point becomes useless and the defensive capabilities of the sword are significantly reduced. Although in swordsmanship the curved sword is used to parry the opponent's strokes, this is a subsidiary objective. It was accepted that parrying was mainly the function of the circular shield. Such a shield was an essential part of the equipment of a soldier from the tenth or eleventh centuries onwards.

Indian sword play favoured cutting and slashing at the opponent, combining it with agility and acrobatics to avoid the enemy's strokes, with the shield always playing an essential part in defence. Some types of daggers, especially the *katar*, are equipped with sword breaking bars descending from the hilt and this indicates that the dagger could also be used for defensive action along with the sword, but this must have been rare.

The shape and the size of the sword was also influenced by whether it was for use by the infantry or the cavalry. The curved sword was ideal for the sweeping cut delivered from the shoulder by the horseman. It was a natural weapon for the purpose.

In the development of European swords, thrusting and the use of the point had more emphasis than the cutting method and use of the edge. Ancient Greek swords were slashing weapons but the shorter Roman swords were intended for thrusting or stabbing. In later centuries, European swords tended to be straight, general purpose weapons. As armour developed and the body was better protected, it became difficult for a sword to cut through with slashes and there was emphasis again on the point for stabbing. Some parts of the body were not adequately protected by armour, such as the armpits or the groin, and it was easier to inflict a wound by thrusting and stabbing rather than by a slashing cut.

In the sixteenth century, a style of sword play was developed in Italy and France which came to be known as fencing. This laid stress entirely on thrusting and the dexterous use of the whole sword for parrying and was very different from the style of swordsmanship prevalent in the Eastern world.

❖ KHANDA BLADE, RAJPUT.

EARLY AND MEDIEVAL
HISTORY OF THE SWORD

P rehistoric man's earliest weapons were made of stone and they were used both for hunting and as weapons of war. He also used wood and bone but only the stone weapons have survived. On the Indian sub-continent such weapons were made out of quartz and included choppers, hand axes, cleavers, spears and arrow heads. These were chipped off from rocks and ground to produce a cutting edge. The hand axes were bound with leather thongs to bone or wooden handles. Spear heads were chipped very thin and bound firmly at the end of the shaft. Stone Age weapons have been found in several parts of the country, with rich hauls from Gujarat, Rajasthan, central India and Madras.

Even though it is difficult to date precisely, it is to Egypt, the fount of so many things, that the first evidence of the sword as a metal-edged weapon can be traced, roughly around 3000 B.C. The sculpture and painting of this period depict several types of swords, daggers and axes in use. In India, the history of the sword can be traced back to the wondrous Indus valley civilization and its two main cities—Mohenjodaro and Harappa, which flourished from 3000 to 1500 B.C.—and coincides with the growth of the ancient civilizations of Egypt, Assyria and Babylonia. The metallic weapons of war that have been excavated at Mohenjodaro include axes, spears, maces, slings, bows and arrows and a few specimens of daggers and swords. These weapons are made of copper as well as bronze. Interestingly, the sword blades are

Facing page

❖ *(Left)* **TALWAR OF MAHARANA HAMIR SINGH, RAJASTHAN, 18TH CENTURY A.D. NATIONAL MUSEUM.** *The hilt differs from the standard Indian hilt in that it has long, slender quillons.*

❖ *(Right)* **SHAMSHEER OF AURANGZEB, MUGHAL, 17TH CENTURY A.D. NATIONAL MUSEUM.** *The pommel (broken) projects to one side and the grip is overlaid with plaques of ivory and has straight, long quillons. On the blade are inscriptions from the Quran in relief.*

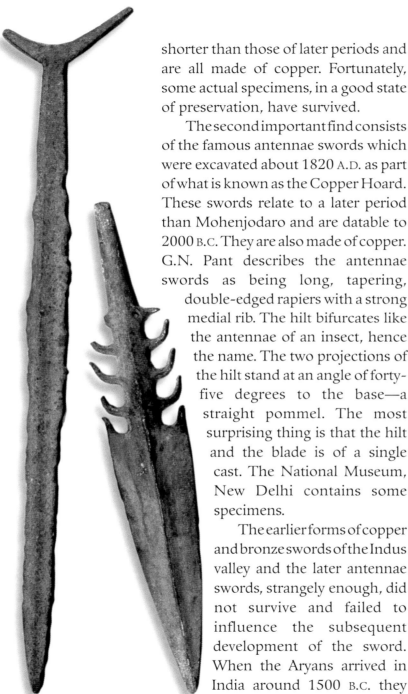

shorter than those of later periods and are all made of copper. Fortunately, some actual specimens, in a good state of preservation, have survived.

The second important find consists of the famous antennae swords which were excavated about 1820 A.D. as part of what is known as the Copper Hoard. These swords relate to a later period than Mohenjodaro and are datable to 2000 B.C. They are also made of copper. G.N. Pant describes the antennae swords as being long, tapering, double-edged rapiers with a strong medial rib. The hilt bifurcates like the antennae of an insect, hence the name. The two projections of the hilt stand at an angle of forty-five degrees to the base—a straight pommel. The most surprising thing is that the hilt and the blade is of a single cast. The National Museum, New Delhi contains some specimens.

The earlier forms of copper and bronze swords of the Indus valley and the later antennae swords, strangely enough, did not survive and failed to influence the subsequent development of the sword. When the Aryans arrived in India around 1500 B.C. they adopted a style and form which was quite different. This is probably because the Aryans brought a different type of sword with them.

With the advent of iron, around 1000 to 800 B.C., copper and bronze gave way to weapons made of iron, as the excavations at Hastinapur (Delhi) show. Copper and bronze are both relatively soft metals and it is difficult to maintain a sharp edge on swords and other weapons made of these metals, but iron being harder retains an edge for a much longer period and is, therefore, more suitable for swords.

The earliest iron swords had two chief forms of blades, both of which, it may be noted, were meant for thrusting and jabbing as opposed to cutting or slashing. The more important form was the leaf shaped, double-edged blade narrowing at the waist and widening near the point. The second type had parallel, straight edges, ending in a short abrupt point. Both sword forms had simple hilts with broad flat pommels.

A variation on the leaf shaped blade is the spoon shaped one, and this was the third form in use. These early swords were, however, basic and functional weapons which served the purpose they were meant to but not completely efficiently.

With the passage of time, weapons became more sophisticated. By medieval times, the Rajputs had developed the *khanda,* which had a broad, straight blade widening slightly towards the point. This was not only elegant but showed highly developed craftsmanship. It is for this reason that the *khanda* has survived into modern times. During this period, aesthetic considerations also started playing a part in sword design and the embellishment of the weapons became important. The development of a superior sword during the medieval period also suggests that the art of swordsmanship had become highly skilled by then.

It is interesting to note that the technical improvements in weapons made during medieval times added not only to the functional properties but also enhanced the aesthetic qualities. This, for example, is true of the reinforcement of the back edge of the blade, like the letter 'T' in section, which, not only strengthened the blade but also added to its aesthetic appeal. Similarly, the knuckle guard which was attached to the hilt protected the hand as it beautified the weapon. Or consider the thickened point of the *katar* (Rajput dagger)—this could pierce chain mail, even while it enhanced the beauty of

the grooved blade. In the *khanda,* the addition of the strengthening ribs along the back edge were in such delicate trellised designs that they added interest and beauty to the weapon. It is clear that medieval swordsmiths were not just skilled

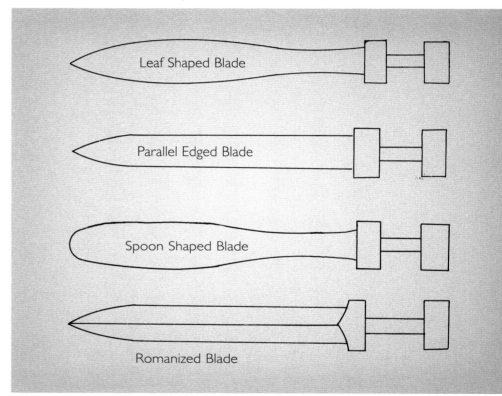

Leaf Shaped Blade

Parallel Edged Blade

Spoon Shaped Blade

Romanized Blade

craftsmen but also artists in their own right.

We can best trace the history of weapons from the specimens that have survived the ravages of time. But from early history, few weapons have

19

...

survived. We have, therefore, to fall back on literary and artistic sources for evidence. Paintings, sculpture, ancient treaties and occasionally numismatics can all be pressed into service to provide supporting evidence, or to fill in our knowledge about periods where no other evidence is available.

❖ RELIEF FROM KHAJURAHO, 10TH AND 11TH CENTURIES A.D. *Depicted here is a parallel edged straight sword.*

With regard to literary sources, the earliest mention of the sword is in the hymns of the *Rig Veda* (1500 B.C.) which is the oldest religious text in the world and one of the earliest written documents. The Aryan civilization, advancing from the Caspian sea and the southern Russian steppes, reached India when the Indus Valley civilization had almost disintegrated, in the second millennium B.C. The hymns of the *Rig Veda*, dedicated to Aryan gods, refer to the *asi* denoting not only the sacrificial sword but also the weapon of war. The *asidhara*, denoting the scabbard, is also mentioned. The *asi* is identified as the chief weapon of the infantry, though the sword together with the spear is also said to be the main weapon of the cavalry.

There is also a passage in the *Mahabharat* which mentions that when a warrior's bows and arrows failed him; when his chariot and charioteer were destroyed; his sword and shield came to his rescue.

Kautilya or Chanakya, author of the *Arthashastra* (320 B.C.), a treatise on government and economics, mentions three types of swords. *Nistrimsa* is described as a sword measuring 30 *angulas* or finger widths. It has a crooked hilt. *Mandalagra* literally means a sword with a round tip instead of a pointed one. The third type of sword mentioned is the *asiyashti* which is described as very sharp and long. Kautilya goes on to add that handles of swords were made of the horns of the rhinoceros and buffalo, of the tusks of elephants, of wood, or of the root of the bamboo. The swords described by Kautiyla find expression in the famous sculptures at Amravati in Andhra and at various other sites.

From the earliest written word about weapons we move on to sculpture for more evidence of their development. One of the earliest representations of the sword in sculpture is from the second century B.C. This is a Buddhist fragment from Bharhut in central India. Another piece is at the great stupa at Sanchi near Bhopal and is datable to the first century A.D. A stupa is a solid domed structure resting on a round base and the one at Sanchi is huge and well-preserved. The sculptures represent incidents from the Buddha's life and the Jataka stories and contain the earliest examples of Buddhist iconography. The standard of technical skill and artistic conception at Sanchi, unlike Bharhut, is extremely high. The great gateways at Sanchi are carved with a multitude of figures and reliefs. Cities are besieged; riders on elephants and horses pass in procession; lions, peacocks and mythical animals roam the jungles. The legend of Prince Siddhartha is represented on one of the bas-reliefs, and is described by Fergusson thus:

When the prince had reached his sixteenth year, his father sought a wife for him among the daughters of the neighbouring rajahs. All refused, however, because the prince, though handsome had not been taught any martial accomplishments and was therefore incapable of controlling women. To prove, however, his power in this respect, he strung a bow that no one else could string, pierced with his arrows thick iron targets at distances none could attain and lastly, shot an arrow an inconceivable distance and where it alighted a spring of water gushed forth which Fa Hien, a great traveller tells us, was later made into a fountain.

At both Bharhut and Sanchi, representations of the sword seem to be similar. Although they are scabbarded these are short swords, about two and a half feet in length, with very broad blades. These blades are straight, double-edged and with rounded tips. The hilts at the two sites differ in detail but show broad circular platform pommels and ring guards. At Sanchi, however, some other carvings also show the leaf shaped blade, to which we have referred earlier. This leaf shaped form later became common all over India.

The next stage in the development of the sword brings us to the sculptures of the first and fourth centuries A.D., executed during the time of the Kushan empire. The Kushans, a Central Asian people from near the western border of China, entered India in the first century A.D. Their empire extended from Gandhara (modern Peshawar) in the north-west to Mathura in the south. It was under Kanishka (about A.D. 78), the greatest of the Kushan kings, that the Kushan empire flowered. Kanishka became a convert to Buddhism and his successors ruled for 150 years.

Culturally, their kingdom was divided into two clearly distinct parts. On the one hand was Gandhara, where the Romano-Egyptian and Romano-Byzantine influence was powerful. On the other was Mathura, where indigenous traditions held the field, though Roman influences from the Indus region and from the north-west occasionally intruded. Rawson notes that the cultural situation is faithfully reflected in the distribution of the weapon types. In Gandhara only Roman sword forms appeared whilst in Mathura the main type is the Indian leaf bladed sword, with the true Roman type appearing occasionally. The Romanized type of sword of the north-west is short, with a centre rib, a hilt with a fairly small platform pommel and a guard that is little more than a band. In contrast, the swords that appear on the Kushan sculptures of Mathura are predominantly of the indigenous leaf bladed type with a hilt, the platform pommel of which is as

Chariots in Warfare

A digression on the use of the chariots in warfare may be of interest. The use of chariots was a totally new concept of fighting that surfaced in the second millennium B.C. For the first time horses were used not as cavalry but to draw chariots carrying armed men. These mobile, armoured, fighting vehicles, when deployed in squadrons and acting together as a disciplined corp, spelt the doom of the ancient formation of pedestrian spearmen.

The *Rig Veda* has an absolutely delightful portrait of Indra and his use of chariots in war: strong-armed, colossal, tawny bearded and pot-bellied from drinking, he wields the thunderbolt in his more god-like moments, but fights like a hero with bows and arrows from his war chariot. He is a cattle raider and a destroyer of the enemy and the victorious leader of the Aryans in their conquest of the hated ancient empire of the Punjab.

Historic evidence shows that chariots ceased to be a branch of the fighting forces by roughly 100 B.C. Greek sources contain an objective and written record of the use of chariots in the battle between Alexander and Porus (326 B.C.), a great and noble north Indian king, on the banks of the river Jhelum. The chariot or the *rath* was the proudest arm of the Indian forces. Each chariot was drawn by four horses and carried six men, namely a shield bearer and an archer on each side, and two drivers armed with javelins. To be able to carry their heavy load of six men with their arms, they had to be heavy wooden structures and consequently could not move fast, unlike the earlier chariots which were smaller, lighter and faster. In the battle against Alexander the Indian chariots proved to be a liability as the heavy rain the night before had turned the ground into a marsh and the chariots, with their enormous weight got stuck in the mud. Others turned over when drivers lashed their horses and tried to make them race over the field. It may, however, be mentioned that this battle was closely fought and according to Plutarch, Alexander's ancient biographer, 'The combat with Porus abated the spirit of Macedonians and made them resolve to proceed no further in India.'

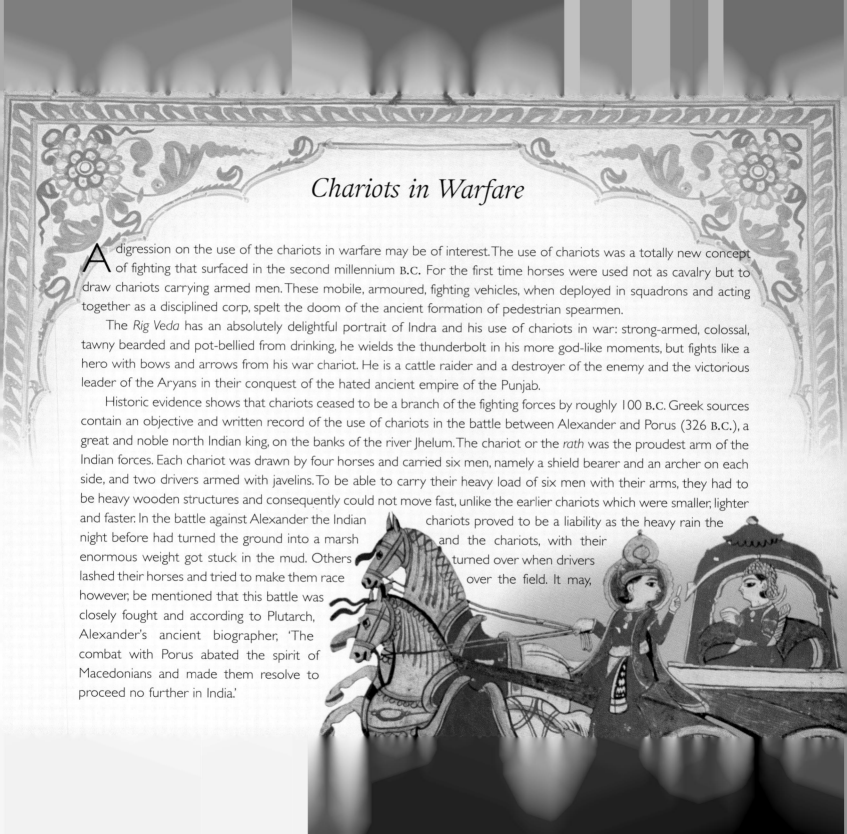

broad as the guard ring fitted to the splayed root of the blade.

The swords excavated at Taxila by the archaeologist John Marshall are dated second century A.D., which is the period we are discussing. These swords are nearly all of the Roman type described above.

There is a remarkable portrait statue of Kanishka at Mathura in which he is shown in Central Asian costume, wearing a long jacket and thick boots and grasping a sword in each hand. The king stands with legs apart in an attitude of authority. Though the head has been broken off, the statue is a work of much power. The two swords represented on it do not belong to an Indian type and probably have a Central Asian pedigree. Both swords are scabbarded and are of longer proportions than was usual in north India at this time.

A frieze in a cave at Udaigiri in Orissa, belonging to the second century A.D. throws more light on the history of the sword, for the swords depicted here are unrelated to the Kushan weapons. The Udaigiri frieze shows a man and a woman fighting with swords. The man wields a long sword with a rounded tip which is very much like the later Rajput *khanda*. The woman is swinging a broad backward curved blade which is not unlike the broad bladed *tegha* of the sixteenth century. Both the *khanda* and the *tegha* reappear several centuries later and although there is no direct evidence of a continuous tradition, it is possible that late medieval sword forms may have had their origins much earlier in history than surmised.

During the period under review, therefore, we have the Romanized type of straight sword with parallel edges in the north-west, and leaf shaped blades which seem to have been in use all over north India.

As I have mentioned earlier, our knowledge of weapons and the armour of early history is tantalizingly vague and uncertain. The history must be pieced together from passing references in texts, from sculpture and paintings. Numismatic evidence is even rarer, but some information on weapons can be gleaned from the coins and inscriptions of Samudra Gupta (335-80 A.D.), one of the most illustrious of the Gupta kings. The Gupta age, also referred to as the classical age of Ancient India, held sway over most of north and central India, going up to Bengal in the east with Pataliputra, modern Patna, as the capital. Samudra Gupta campaigned as far south as Kanchipuram, near

Madras, and although the kings in the south were not under Gupta suzerainty, they were forced to pay homage. Many inscriptions of Samudra Gupta are on gold coins as well as on a stone pillar now housed in Allahabad fort. The coins show a variety of weapons and the inscriptions on them mention the remarkable qualities of Samudra Gupta, for whom the wounds of battle were marks of beauty and honour. Inscribed in Sanskrit, rather than the Prakrit or Pali used earlier, the epithets read: he was a fearless fighter and brave as a tiger *(vyaghra - parakrami)*; the hero of a hundred battles *(samrasata)*, which left on his body their scars *(vrana)* as marks of decoration *(sobha)* and beauty *(kanti)*, scars of various kinds caused by the different weapons of war *(praharana)*, such as *parasu* (battle-axe), *sara* (arrow) *sanku* (spear), *sakti* (spike) *prasa* (barbed dart), *asi* (sword), *tomara* (iron club), *bhindipala* (javelin) *naracha* (iron arrow) and *vaitastika* (scimitar). The king depended on his personal prowess as his only ally *(swabhuja bala-parakramaika-bandhoh)*.

Interestingly, Samudra Gupta also revived the horse sacrifice or *asvamedha*, which was an ancient practice, where a special horse was permitted to wander at will and the king claimed all territory over which it wandered. Stopping the horse meant immediate war. The *asvamedha* coins show a horse wearing a breast band and standing before an altar from which a banner flies over the horse's back. The coins carry the legend, 'the king of kings having conquered the earth now conquers heaven with invincible valour by celebrating the *asvamedha* sacrifice.'

The swords of this period appear in sculptures in the Udaigiri cave in Orissa and the Khandagiri hill. The earlier leaf bladed and spoon bladed swords continue to be depicted in these sculptures, but with definite technical improvements. Gupta swords represent a significant step towards the

❖ EARLY SOUTH INDIAN SWORD, E. JAIWANT PAUL COLLECTION
Sword with a flexible blade and bells attached to the edges. Used for religious and domestic ceremonies.

Facing page

❖ EARLY SOUTH INDIAN SWORD, E. JAIWANT PAUL COLLECTION
The quillons are turned up. The blade is straight and continuously tapering.

development of later weapons. The swords are longer, more slender and proportionate and suggest that a superior quality of metal was in use. The hilt also shows more sophistication, with the grip bulging the Gupta sculptures may be considered to be the precursors of the later *khanda*.

Between the seventh and twelfth centuries many regional states were established in north India. Three main

in the middle and narrowing at the upper and lower ends, a feature characteristic of the modern hilt and which may be termed the standard Indian hilt. The weapons depicted on powers vied for the control of Kanauj, the imperial city. These were the Rashtrakutas from the Deccan, the Pratiharas from Rajasthan and the Palas. Each gained prominence and power for a time. The Pratiharas and the Rashtrakutas successfully resisted the Arabs and restricted them to the largely uninhabited desert area of Sind.

The Palas, who controlled Bengal and Bihar, were Buddhists. Many

Throughout this period, swords show no development or progress and seem to have regressed towards older types. Pala swords are generally short and have thick blades, unlike the slender and superior Gupta swords. At the same

images and paintings of Buddhist deities from the Pala school survive and a large number of these show deities holding symbolic swords and it is from these that conclusions are drawn.

time, however, ornamentation makes an appearance for the first time, though most of it is nonfunctional. Remarking on the Pala swords, Rawson comments: Pala swords follow only the two main

The Battle of Tarain

Under the leadership of Prithviraj, the Rajput chieftains fought against Muhammad Ghori of Afghanistan, who was trying to wrest the lordship of Hindustan. Sir Jadunath Sarkar the eminent historian, gives a lively account of this great battle, fought in 1191 at Tarain: The battle joined as the Hindus gave the signal for attack by blowing conch shells from the backs of elephants, while the Turks struck their kettledrums carried on camels and sounded their trumpets. The impetuous charge of the Rajputs scattered like a cloud the Muslim vanguard.

Advancing further, they attacked both wings of the Turkish army and inclining inwards dispersed their opponents and threatened the centre, where the Sultan commanded in person. Large numbers of his horsemen began to slip away, not daring to face the roaring tide of Rajput cavalry flushed with victory. The Sultan was urged to save himself by flight as he had no support left. But, scorning such cowardly counsel, he made a reckless charge into the body of Rajputs before him, hewing his way with his sword and followed by a small body of devoted companions. Govind Rai (the governor of Delhi) who led the vanguard of his brother Prithviraj, on sighting Ghori from a distance, drove his elephant towards him. The two met in single combat. The Sultan's lance knocked out two of Govind Rai's front teeth, while the Indian chief hurled a javelin which inflicted a severe wound on the upper arm of Ghori and forced him to turn his horse's head round in agony and weakness. However, he was saved from falling down by a Khalj youth who leaped upon his horse from behind and kept him on the saddle with his arms and, urging the horse on by word of mouth, carried him away to the base in safety.

The rout of the Turkish army was complete, but such a victory did not yield its full fruits as the Rajputs were incapable of making a relentless pursuit and their country-bred ponies were outpaced by the Khurasani horses of the Turkish army.

The Sultan set himself to avenge this defeat. He raised a vast force of Turks and Afghans estimated at 120,000 cavalry clad in armour (*Tabaqat-i-Nasir*). The Indian army was much smaller than in the first battle, as Prithviraj had delayed in mobilizing his forces. Many of his former allies did not join him and his long-term rival, Jaichand, the Raja of Kanauj, traitorously allied himself with Ghori. The second battle, also fought at Tarain, was a complete victory for the Turks.

History books say that Prithviraj was slain in the battle. Chand Bardai, the famous bard of Rajasthan, in his 100,000 verse epic *Prithviraj Raso,* to which we have referred earlier, states that Prithviraj was not killed in battle, but was captured

by Ghori, taken to Afghanistan, blinded, and kept there. Prithviraj's prowess as an archer was legendary and though blinded, he could still find his aim if given an indication of direction and distance. Sultan Ghori once asked Prithviraj to demonstrate his archery to visitors from north India among whom was Chand Bardai. Just as Prithviraj was about to start, Chand recited a couplet:

Char bans, chaubis gaz, ungal asht pramaan
Ta uchyo baitha hai Sultan, mat chukyo Chauhan.

This gave Prithviraj the direction and distance at which Sultan Ghori sat. Chand added that if you are a Chauhan you will not miss him. Whereupon Prithviraj swung around and shot the arrow straight through Ghori's chest.

Few history books mention this version but I was astonished to find evidence for this story in Afghanistan. Some years ago, I was driving from Kabul to Kandhar and passed through Ghazni with its mud fort. On the outskirts of Ghazni I espied two domed tombs. Having stopped and made enquiries, I discovered that the larger tomb was that of Sultan Ghori and a few metres away was a second smaller tomb. In the centre of the second tomb was a bare patch of earth, where the actual grave should have been. Hanging over this spot from the top of the dome was a long, thick rope ending in a knot at shoulder height. Local visitors would grab hold of this knot in one hand and stamp vigorously and repeatedly with one foot on the bare patch in the centre of the tomb. I watched this happen several times and seeking an explanation for this strange routine, I discovered the astounding fact that this was the tomb of Prithviraj Chauhan. The Afghans still stamped on his grave because he killed Ghori, 900 years ago. Prithviraj's tomb stands near Ghazni and history books need to be rewritten. That day a flower was placed on that bare patch of earth, but it must have soon been stamped upon.

His remains must be brought back home, where they belong.

forms of the early Indian swords, the leaf bladed and the straight parallel edged. The tips of both types are rounded. The pommel of the hilt of all the swords is always a broad circular platform and the guard is most frequently a thick ring but fairly often the root of the blade is splayed out into a guard that looks like the duofoil of the old Indian hilt. No Pala sculpture or paintings show scabbards and this would suggest that naked swords were carried in the hand.

In the ninth and tenth centuries, the Rajputs enter the scene. They were of Scythic origin and the cradle of the race has been variously described as 'amidst the hills of the Caucasus and the steppes of Central Asia.' Of the various clans of Rajputs, thirty-six in all, the Chauhans established themselves in eastern Rajasthan and the Tomars in the Haryana region. The city of Dhillika (Delhi) was founded by them about 800 A.D. The Parmar clan ruled Malwa and the Chandellas the area around Khajuraho.

During the eleventh and twelfth centuries, the Rajput clans fought each other increasingly. The possession of kingdom became a precarious business and the competition for territory a perpetual activity. War became a part of the general chivalric code, even a sport. Warring regional chiefs were known to dine with each other after a hard day's battle and decide on the time to start the next day, rather like war were a game of cricket!

Prithviraj Raso, an epic poem composed by the bard Chand Bardai, describes the life and times of the last Chauhan king of Delhi and Ajmere, Prithviraj (late 12th century). It also gives a description of the arms and armour of the early medieval era in north India. The types of swords mentioned in the *Prithviraj Raso* are enumerated by M.L. Nigam as the *khadga, tegha, lohatti, vaddhali* (sharp-edged sword), *dodhara* (double-edged sword), *niraasi* (sword with watered blade), *patta*, south Indian *katti* and the *gupti* (sword stick). The daggers mentioned are the *jamadhara (yamadhra), hari hetha* (lion's paw), *katar* and *chhuri*. These names are Sanskritized and suggest their indigenous origins. *Prithviraj Raso*, therefore, describes the traditional weapons in India before the advent of Central Asian or Persian weapons.

The major evidence for the history of the sword in the eleventh and twelfth centuries is gleaned from the sculpture at the Nilakanteshwar temple at Kekind in Rajasthan, the Harshnath temple at Sikar, also in Rajasthan and from the great Chandela city of Khajuraho.

At the Nilakanteshwar and Khajuraho temples, swords which are similar in most respects appear. The blades narrow mid-point, at the waist, and are spoon shaped with rounded tips. In addition, the blades have a centre ridge. The hilts have broad, circular, platform pommels, surmounted by a knob. Others have pommels shaped like domes, again surmounted by a knob.

The Khajuraho temples were built in the tenth and eleventh centuries by the kings of Bundelkhand, who were Rajputs of the Chandela clan. It is worth describing briefly some of the other swords depicted at Khajuraho although they may not directly follow the line of development of the sword which we have been pursuing. A myriad varieties of swords appear on these beautiful temples: double-edged straight swords, thrust swords, cut swords, even curved swords. Great military processions show soldiers with arms stretched downwards, carrying swords in a horizontal position. Hunting scenes abound, showing hunters on foot and others mounted on horseback, carrying or using swords and spears. Interestingly, women are shown wielding swords or carrying swords, daggers and bows.

At the Harshnath temple at Sikar there is a representation of a long sword, again with a ridged *khanda* blade. The hilt of this blade is similar to the Khajuraho and the Nilakanteshwar swords mentioned earlier. These representations, further supplemented by the Jain miniatures of the time, would suggest that this is the classical pre-Islamic Rajput sword, the direct ancestor of the Rajput *khanda*. Some ornamentation in relief is also shown.

A second group of swords that are seen on a relief at Harshnath needs special mention as the swords represented here are ones with forward angled blades and are encountered for the first time. The forward edge is curved and the reverse edge is sharply angled forward.

This sword is important not only because it is a southern type but is also deemed by some authorities to be the ancestor of the weapons used by the Rajputs like the *sosun patta* and the Nepalese *kukri* (both dealt with later).

Having considered literary sources and sculpture, we next move on to paintings in tracing the history of weapons. The Ajanta cave paintings and the later Jain manuscript

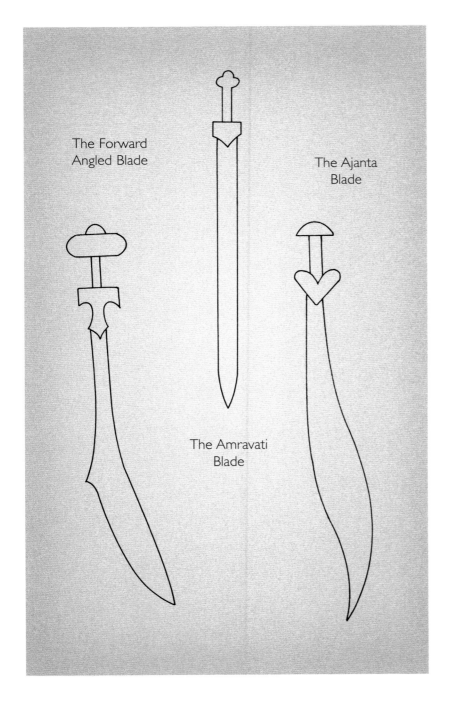

The Forward
Angled Blade

The Ajanta
Blade

The Amravati
Blade

paintings of the tenth century are of special relevance. The Mughal and Rajput miniatures of the different schools or *kalams* painted between 1550 and 1800 A.D. provide splendid material for tracing the development of the sword. This is particularly so, as in many miniatures there was a great deal of emphasis on portraiture and the depiction of the rich brocades, sword and daggers which were the essential accoutrement of the aristocracy. But again some confusion is created by the fact that weapons shown in the miniatures of around 1600 A.D. sometimes differ hardly at all from those seen in photographs taken by the well-known court photographer of Hyderabad, Raja Deen Dayal, as late as the 1870s. Says Rawson, of this period:

In the medieval period in western India, the Rajput *khanda* and the standard Indian (or Indo-Muslim) hilt were developed. The sword with the forward angled blade is also encountered. The members of the hilt are often accorded plastic ornamentation, indicating the growth of the native Indian interest in the aesthetic expression of the sword. Elegance in the forms of the blade is clearly sought after.

THE SWORD IN SOUTH INDIA

~

Although the main swords of the north were prevalent in the earlier centuries in the south, in the medieval and late medieval periods certain divergent trends can be traced.

The earliest evidence is found in the hoard of iron swords found at Adichalanur in the Trinulvelli district. The dates of these weapons are approximately second or first century B.C. The types found here follow the earliest north Indian swords which include the leaf-shaped blades and the parallel sided blades. In addition, a third type is the straight and continuously tapering blade which was not found in the north at the time. All the swords have prominent central ridges and are longer than the north Indian variety. Most of these swords also have a spike on top of the hilt.

In the second and third centuries A.D. many sculptured representations of the sword are found on Buddhist monuments at Amravati in Andhra. C. Sivaramamurthy, in the *Bulletin of the Madras Museum*, lists the various types found here as the lotus petal shaped sword, the bamboo leaf shaped sword, the *mangalagra* type found in the raised hand of a soldier and the *asiyasti*, a very long, sharp sword mentioned by Kautilya. The tips of the swords are of three types: flat, rounded and curviconical. Small daggers are also represented in the sculptures and these are called *churrikas*. Some sheaths and straps are also depicted but they all appear to be made of leather. A type found predominantly at Amravati is the straight, narrow blade, double-edged sword with parallel sides. The contours of this sword are slender and different from other swords of the time.

Strangely, for the next three hundred years there is no further light on the sword in the south till we come to the Buddhist caves at Ajanta in the sixth century A.D. The term cave is a misnomer because some of the halls at Ajanta are huge and imposing, imitating structural buildings.

The tradition of murals in cave shrines started some time in the first century A.D. The paintings in the

❖ **RAJPUT MINIATURE PAINTING.**
Army on the march. Note the magnificent attire of the Raja on the elephant and the horsemen.

twenty-nine caves that comprise Ajanta date from the second century A.D. and go right upto the seventh century, and therefore these frescoes furnish a record that covers a vast span of time. The finest paintings at Ajanta, however, date to Vataka, of whom little is known, and Chalukya patronage in the fifth and sixth centuries A.D. The frescoes mainly illustrate the Jatakas, which recount incidents from the previous incarnations of the Buddha, while other paintings represent secular subjects, court life and the deeds of kings.

Many weapons are represented in these murals and the sword has been painted numerous times. There are long and short swords with straight, double-edged blades, as well as ornate ones with long and slender proportions. The hilts have angular V-shaped guards; some are jewelled and highly embellished. There are swords with ornate sheaths and others carried naked in the hands of soldiers. As would be expected, all Ajanta swords are elegantly proportioned and beautifully painted.

Some of the sword types suggest the north Indian *khanda* with a waisted blade and rounded tip, the main sword type in use in north India at this time. There are yet others with the kopis blade, which is narrow near the root, gradually broadens and curves forward, attains its greatest width near the point, and then recurves. One can also see from the proportions of the Ajanta swords that by this time the craft of the swordsmith has become highly developed.

Other evidence of the sword is from the rock cut temples of Ellora in Maharashtra and the Mahaballipuram sculptures near Madras, both of which were executed around the seventh and eight centuries A.D. At this time the main dynasties in south India were the Pallavas in Tamil Nadu, their sworn enemies the Chalukyas in Karnataka, and the Rashtrakutas in north Deccan, who served as a bridge between north and south India and enabled an interchange of ideas and culture.

At Ellora and Mahabalipuram are seen the two chief Indian blades—the

❖ SOUTH INDIAN DAGGER, MYSORE, 18TH CENTURY A.D., E. JAIWANT PAUL COLLECTION.

leaf-shaped and the straight parallel-edged type. The hilts have simple guard collars. The kopis blade, considered by Rawson to be the direct ancestor of the south Indian flamboyant sword, is also seen occasionally.

Interesting evidence on the development of the sword is provided by Indian kingdoms, who had established colonies in South East Asia as early as the second century A.D. Some of these colonies lasted for more than a thousand years, long after the end of Hindu rule in India. In the ninth century A.D., a Hindu dynasty founded by Sailendra constructed the famous stupa of Borobudur in Java and to this day it stands as a living monument of the grandeur and magnificence of this dynasty. Situated on top of a hill, the stupa consists of a series of nine successive terraces, each receding from the one beneath it, the whole crowned by a bell shaped stupa at the centre of the top-most terrace.

There are a large number of reliefs showing palaces and soldiers holding a vast range of sword types used by the Indian colonialist. These sword forms of the ninth century represent an essential step in the development of the south Indian sword. At this stage the swords are practical weapons of war and have not acquired the later

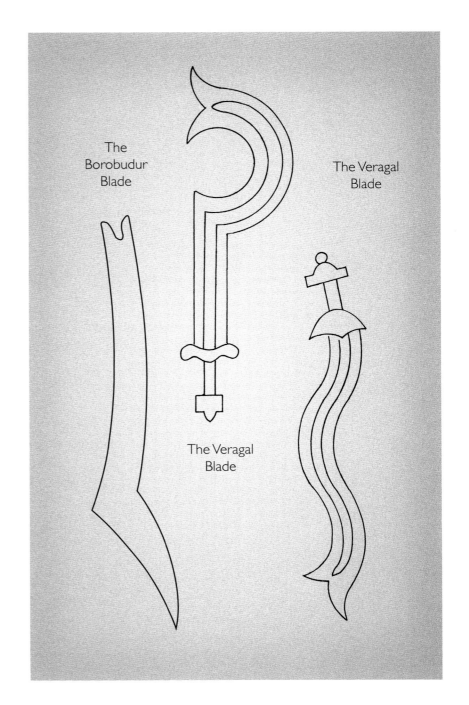

The
Borobudur
Blade

The Veragal
Blade

The Veragal
Blade

extravagant forms that actually impaired the utility and fighting capacity of the weapons.

The commonest representation at Borobudur is the long, straight, spoon bladed sword which closely resembles the *khanda*. The pommel is a large circular cushion, usually surmounted by a dome or bead. The guard is in the form of long ears with downward scrolled tips. The other blade of importance is the double curved heavy sword which has been earlier referred to as the kopis type. Another blade form is the curved one with the sharply forward angled reverse edge. The Indian colonists did not adopt any indigenous weapons of Java, as they were primitive.

The swords seen at the Veragal tombstones of military heroes near Mysore, datable to 960 A.D., are clearly of a form which would post them as the ancestors of what has been termed as the south Indian flamboyant sword. However, there are others which have fantastic forms and more visual ferocity than actual practical value. There are sickle shaped swords bifurcated at the point and serpentine swords also ending in two points. These shapes would actually impede their use as fighting swords and suggest that swordsmanship must have been a neglected art at this time. What were in earlier weapons, slight angularities and gentle curves become in this period marked angles and deep curves.

The Vijayanagar (modern Hampi) empire was established in 1336 A.D. and lasted almost three hundred years. Under Krishnadeva Raja the empire covered most of the southern peninsula, including Madurai in the south and Goa in the west. It had to its credit brilliant cultural and artistic achievements but a taste for over embellishment and extravagance seems to have been acquired too. However, this trait is difficult to reconcile with Vijayanagar's need for technically efficient weapons as it had an almost unbroken record of conflict with its neighbours over three centuries; conflicts that could hardly be pursued with impractical weapons. Unfortunately, there is not much more information on Vijayanagar weaponry.

In the medieval age the south Indian sword took on an extravagance of form which must often have sorely impeded its proper use. There was a great variety of blade shapes: straight, undulating, hooked, bellied, curved and elbowed, most of which seem to be the product of individual invention, and their forms must be regarded as products of fantasy rather than practical use.

However, the most important sword of the south was the flamboyant sword. Rawson observes that this sword was made in several versions. All have the upward inclined quatrefoil guard and a large composite pommel, often with a wooden cushion.

The sword is highly ornate with a blade that is a combination of the forward angle and the kopis form with a root that splays out to a width far greater than that of the belly of the blade. The seating is very elaborately worked, graven and chiselled, either forming a part of the hilt or being a separate member attached by rivets to both hilt and blade.

Finally, a word about Nair temple swords. Their construction is such that they could not have been used for fighting. There are swords with flexible blades that vibrate for a considerable time and others with bells attached to the edges of the blades and in the hollows of the pommels. These are used for domestic and other ceremonies and need not be covered here in any detail.

❖ SOUTH INDIAN DAGGER, E. JAIWANT PAUL COLLECTION. *With a double curved blade, this small dagger has an ornate hilt.*

THE LAST FIVE CENTURIES

THE MUGHALS

From about the thirteenth century A.D. to the advent of the Mughals in the sixteenth century A.D., very little is available concerning the development of the sword in India. During this period the Turks and Afghans had established themselves in north-west India and it can be assumed that the influence of Persian armourers, who had acquired a worldwide reputation, was dominant in the north.

Persian swordsmiths were often employed at the principal Indian courts and by the sixteen-hundreds, Indian swordsmiths and craftsmen had fully mastered the Persian techniques, so that it became difficult to say whether a weapon or piece of armour was Indian or Persian in origin. The Persian sword was curved backward, and while this had appeared in Persia much earlier, its adoption and use in India dates to the fifteenth and sixteenth centuries.

A large haul of actual weapons of the Mughal era is from the reign of Akbar (1556-1605 A.D.), though it is often not possible to date them accurately. The quality and nature of the blade and the character and extent of the ornamentation on the hilt and the blade are good indications. However, other important guides are the miniature paintings of the Mughal and Rajput schools, which flourished almost contemporaneously from 1550 to 1800 A.D. It may be mentioned that Mughal art was the result of the fusion of Persian and Rajput styles of painting. While Mughal painting remained a court art largely patronized by the aristocracy, Rajput painting was a folk

Facing page

❖ TALWAR OF TIPU SULTAN, KARNATAKA, 1790 A.D., NATIONAL MUSEUM.
The standard Indian hilt is damascened in gold and the blade is inscribed in gold.

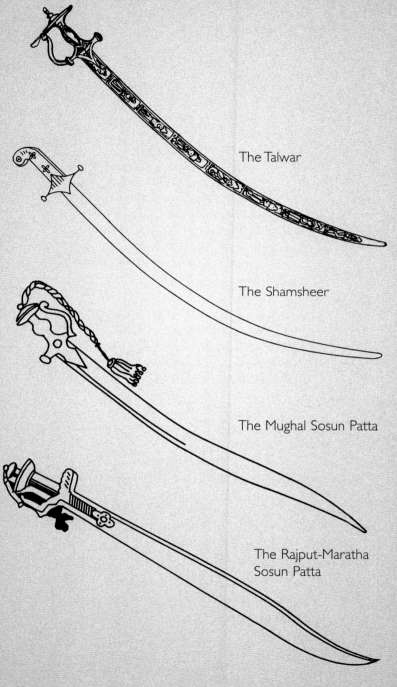

The Talwar

The Shamsheer

The Mughal Sosun Patta

The Rajput-Maratha
Sosun Patta

art, produced by the people for their own pleasure and edification. Both were inclined to portraiture and it is this, as well as paintings of battle and hunting scenes, that provide a key to our quest for swords and daggers. The paintings resolved into various styles or *kalams*, which represented regional variations, and this further helps in identifying weapons from different regions.

It is necessary to distinguish between the *talwar* and the *shamsheer*. The *talwar* became the most popular sword in the country and was used both by the Mughals and the Rajputs of the north, though in southern Rajasthan, central India and Orissa, the *khanda* continued in use. The *talwar* has a curved blade, although there may be considerable variation in size, curvature and quality. It also tends to be of uniform width from the root till it nears the point or *nok*. The curvature of the blade favours the cutting and slashing method of use. The hilt is the standard Indian hilt which is sometimes termed the Indo-Muslim hilt. It has a button on top, a circular flat pommel, a grip which narrows at the top and bottom and thickens in the middle, short heavy quillons and small langets. Some hilts have knuckle guards, while others do not. *Talwars* generally have the ricasso *(khazana)*, or the short blunt portion on the edge near the hilt, to safeguard the index finger, which is sometimes hooked round the blade below the quillon. The ricasso was never found on *shamsheers*.

The *shamsheer*, which is Persian in origin but found widespread use in India, has a blade with a deeper curve. This renders its point almost useless but makes it a perfect cutting and slashing weapon. The blade is narrow, thick and continuously tapering from the root to the point, unlike the *talwar* blade which is the same width through most of its length. The hilt is pistol shaped with the pommel projecting to one side, sometimes covered with a metal cap or an embellishment. The grip is straight and simple. The cross guard has long slender quillons. Knuckle guards are rarely seen on *shamsheer* hilts. The smaller version of the shamsheer is called the *nimcha* and may have been meant for the use of children.

A vast variety of *talwars* and *shamsheers* are available in the major museums and in private collections. The most valued have been made by the celebrated swordsmith Assadullah of Isfahan. Unfortunately, both in India and Persia, where the practice of signing blades prevailed, many fake signatures of this renowned swordsmith are to be found.

The *sosun patta* means lily leaf and refers to the shape of the blade which has the kopis form, popular in many countries. It has a slightly narrow portion near the root, the blade widens and curves forward, broadens near the tip and then recurves and runs to a point. The word kopis and the type of blade it represents—the forward curved blade—is Egyptian in origin, and goes as far back as the Pharoahs. Rawson says, the classification kopis covers the Turkish and the Balkan sword called the *yataghan*, the Nepalese *kukri*, the *sosun patta* and the south Indian flamboyant sword. Blades of pure kopis form appear in India in the sixth century at Ajanta and persist into modern times.

The two versions of the *sosun patta*, the Mughal and the Rajput-Maratha, have some minor variations. The Mughal *sosun patta* has the standard Indian hilt, while the Rajput-Maratha has the basket type of hilt.

The *tegha* was used by the Mughals, Marathas and the Rajputs. It seems to be of northern Hindu origin. The

❖ SOSUN PATTA, NATIONAL MUSEUM.
The blade here has the kopis form, slightly narrow near the root, curving forward, recurving and running to a point.

43

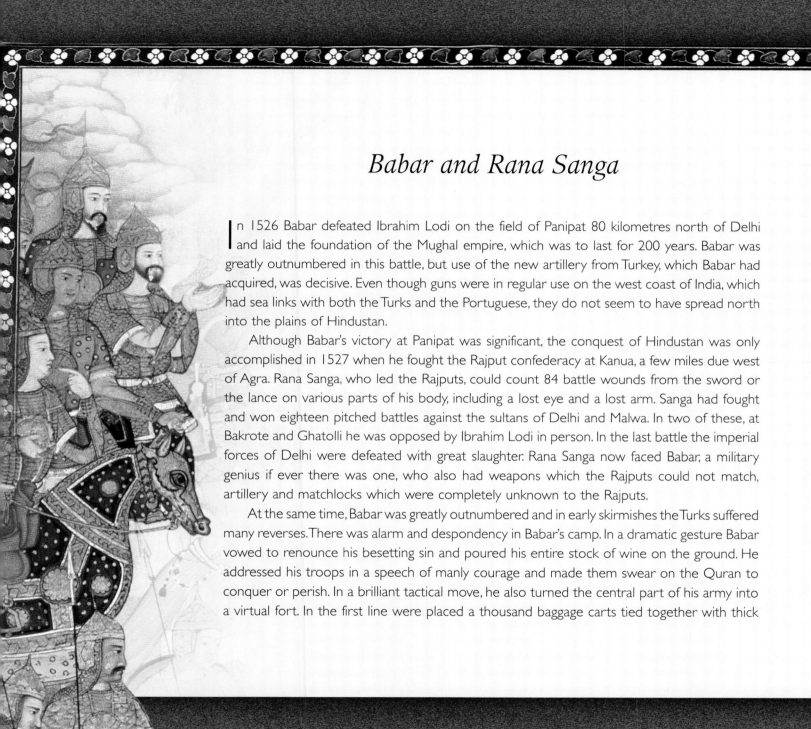

Babar and Rana Sanga

In 1526 Babar defeated Ibrahim Lodi on the field of Panipat 80 kilometres north of Delhi and laid the foundation of the Mughal empire, which was to last for 200 years. Babar was greatly outnumbered in this battle, but use of the new artillery from Turkey, which Babar had acquired, was decisive. Even though guns were in regular use on the west coast of India, which had sea links with both the Turks and the Portuguese, they do not seem to have spread north into the plains of Hindustan.

Although Babar's victory at Panipat was significant, the conquest of Hindustan was only accomplished in 1527 when he fought the Rajput confederacy at Kanua, a few miles due west of Agra. Rana Sanga, who led the Rajputs, could count 84 battle wounds from the sword or the lance on various parts of his body, including a lost eye and a lost arm. Sanga had fought and won eighteen pitched battles against the sultans of Delhi and Malwa. In two of these, at Bakrote and Ghatolli he was opposed by Ibrahim Lodi in person. In the last battle the imperial forces of Delhi were defeated with great slaughter. Rana Sanga now faced Babar, a military genius if ever there was one, who also had weapons which the Rajputs could not match, artillery and matchlocks which were completely unknown to the Rajputs.

At the same time, Babar was greatly outnumbered and in early skirmishes the Turks suffered many reverses. There was alarm and despondency in Babar's camp. In a dramatic gesture Babar vowed to renounce his besetting sin and poured his entire stock of wine on the ground. He addressed his troops in a speech of manly courage and made them swear on the Quran to conquer or perish. In a brilliant tactical move, he also turned the central part of his army into a virtual fort. In the first line were placed a thousand baggage carts tied together with thick leather thongs but with some gaps in between for the horsemen to sally forth. The cannons and the foot musketeers formed the second line behind the carts. In the third stood the heavy cavalry.

Wave upon wave of Rajput cavalry could not break through Babar's fortress-like centre. The artillery played havoc in the close ranks of the charging cavalry. Thoroughly bewildered by the thunder and lightning of cannons, as they had never seen anything like this before, the Rajputs shifted their attention to Babar's right and left flanks, which were unsupported by artillery and met with considerable success. While the outcome of the battle still hung in the balance, Silhadi, a Rajput turned Muslim, defected with his contingent to Babar's side and upset Sanga's plan of combat. Disaster struck again when Sanga lost consciousness because of a severe wound. To keep the troops from being demoralized, a counterfeit Sanga was seated on the royal elephant. The Rajputs, convulsed and decimated by cannon and matchlock, then set out on the famous death ride which ended in their decimation.

distinction between the *tegha* and *talwar* is very narrow and only a sword with a very broad blade, deeply curved backward can be termed the *tegha*. It sometimes has the Hindu basket hilt.

Another sword seen during this period was the *pulouar*, which also has a curved blade. The quillons, drooping downwards, have enlarged, pierced and fretted ends. The pommel is a pierced, covered ball surmounted by a cone. The grip is generally chiselled. It probably has an Arabic pedigree.

Abul Fazal, Akbar's friend and adviser, in his two great chronicles of the reign of Akbar, the *Akbar Nama* and *Ain-i-Akbari*, provides a full and detailed account of Akbar's life and times. Abul Fazal describes Akbar's arms thus:

All weapons for the use of His Majesty have names and proper rank is assigned to them. Thus, there are thirty swords (*khasa* swords) one of which is sent daily to His Majesty's sleeping apartments. The old one is returned and handed over to the servants outside the harem who keep it till its turn comes again. Forty other swords are kept in readiness: they are called *kotal* swords and when necessary replace the *khasa* swords.

He goes on to say that Akbar practised with his sword every day. Sixty-nine weapons in use are listed and include, curved swords, the *khada* (straight sword), *gupti saca* (sword stick), *jamdhar* (broad dagger), *khanjar, jambua, katar, karad,* etc. The *Ain-i-Akbari* states that the price of a sword ranged from half a rupee to fifteen *muhars* or gold coins.

The aesthetic development of the Indian sword reached its zenith during the Mughal period. Mughal emperors often presented silk and brocade robes, valuable swords and daggers for loyal service or as recognition of delegated authority. A fine sword or dagger at the belt of a courtier indicated his position at the court and signalled imperial approval. This practice further encouraged the demand for ornamented weapons.

Ideally, embellishment and ornamentation should increase the

❖ **PULOUAR, MUGHAL, 18TH CENTURY A.D., NATIONAL MUSEUM.** *The quillons droop downward, and the grooved blade is slightly curved.*

aesthetic appeal of the weapon, but not impede its function. Good quality *talwars*, *shamsheers*, as well as the Rajput *khanda*, the Maratha *pata* and many other sword forms, developed a variety of ornamentation on the hilt and the blade. These included inlay and application of gold and silver to steel and iron. This is sometimes referred to as damascening, and with some changes in technique it becomes *koftgari*. Enamelling was also done wherein a pigmented glaze is made to adhere to a metal surface. Gilding involved the application of gold leaf to a surface which had been previously cross hatched with a graver or prepared to receive it by the use of acid. Jewelling was done on the hilt and precious stones, including emeralds and rubies, were studded and encrusted with gold, giving an effect of abounding richness. Chiselling was also practised with ornamental forms graved into the metal surface. By a special process this could also be done in relief with the design standing out. Bidri work was done on hilts and this involved the inlay of silver on a black background of alloy.

Hilts were often made entirely of jade, cornelian or other semi-precious stones. These were enriched with gold inlay. Elephant and walrus ivory was also used for hilts.

Apart from decoration, one needs to touch briefly on the watered blade so popular around this time. In high quality blades a watered effect, showing a pattern of wavy lines or circular knot-like designs, was often found. This was confused with damascening, the art of inlaying gold, silver and occasionally copper wire on the surface of the iron or steel blade of a sword. Damascus had a reputation for the manufacture of the finest steel weapons but in all probability the metal from which the ancient blades of Damascus were made was brought from India. Indian steel or *wootz* was exported from Kutch to the ports of the Persian Gulf. The pattern in the Indian steel blades of this period was produced by the old Indian steel preparation method. Hot

❖ GUPTI, RAJASTHAN, EARLY 19TH CENTURY A.D., NATIONAL MUSEUM. *The narrow blade fits into a painted wooden sheath, thus disguising it as a walking stick.*

Chittorgarh

The rite of *jauhar* has been performed three times at Chittor. First in 1303 during Allauddin Khilji's siege, next in 1535 against the Sultan of Gujarat and finally in 1567 when Akbar besieged the fort. The 1303 episode had such elements of drama that it bears repetition. Padmini, the queen of Rana Rattan Singh of Mewar, was the daughter of Hamir Chauhan of Sri Lanka. Her exquisite beauty, many accomplishments and final destruction constitute the subject of one of the most popular traditions of *rajwarra*. According to the great bard, Chand Bardai, Allauddin Khilji's invasion of Mewar was prompted as much by his desire for territorial expansion as his infatuation with Padmini. After a long and fruitless siege of Chittor, Allauddin sent word to Rana Rattan Singh that he would depart, if only he could behold Padmini's extraordinary beauty. This the Rana was not willing to accept but it was finally agreed that Allauddin could behold her reflection through a series of mirrors. Relying on the good faith of Rattan Singh, Allauddin entered Chittor lightly guarded, and having gratified his wish, returned. Rattan Singh, not to be outdone in confidence, accompanied the king to the foot of the fortress, where he was ambushed and made prisoner. Word was sent that Rattan Singh's liberty was dependent on the surrender of Padmini. A scheme was devised by the Rajputs and word dispatched to Allauddin that Padmini would surrender, but in a manner befitting her high station, she would arrive accompanied by her handmaidens and friends; not only those who would accompany her to Delhi but others who wanted to pay their last respects. Allauddin was strictly warned against violating the sanctity of female decorum and privacy. No less than seven hundred covered litters proceeded to Allauddin's camp. In each was placed one of the bravest defenders of Chittor, borne by six armed soldiers disguised as litter porters. On reaching the camp, in strict privacy, a last meeting between the Rana and Padmini was permitted. The Rana was placed in a litter and the devoted warriors, emerging from the litters, covered his retreat to the fort till they perished to a man.

Allauddin, defeated in his objective, was obliged to retreat. But having recovered his strength, he returned to Chittor in 1303. Rattan Singh had not yet recovered the loss of so many valiant men who had sacrificed themselves for their king's safety and Allauddin carried on his attack more closely. When further resistance against the organized strength of

the Delhi army seemed impossible, the Rajputs preferred death to disgrace and here I quote James Tod: 'but another awful sacrifice was to precede this act of self devotion, in that horrible rite of jauhar where the females are immolated to preserve them from pollution or captivity. The funeral pyre was lighted within the great subterranean retreat, in chambers impervious to the light of day and the defenders of Chittor beheld in procession the queens, their own wives and daughters to the number of several thousands. The fair Padmini closed the thong and they were conveyed to the cavern and the opening closed upon them, leaving them to find security from dishonour in the devouring fire.'

The Rana then called his devoted clans, for whom life no longer held any charms. They threw open the portals and descended to the plains and with reckless despair carried death or met it in the crowded ranks of Allauddin. The Tatar conqueror took possession of an inanimate capital, strewed with brave defenders, the smoke still issuing from the recesses where lay consumed the once fair object of his desire. And since this day the cavern has been sacred: no eye has penetrated its gloom. Thus fell the celebrated capital in the round of conquest of Khilji, one of the most vigorous and warlike sovereigns who have occupied the throne of India.

crumbled iron was reheated in a crucible, with charcoal round it. After a considerable time the iron became partly recarbonized. When it was drawn out on the anvil as steel, it showed a beautiful pattern of lines through the crystallization of the metal. This is called the watering effect *(jauhar)*. Various patterns emerge on the blade when watered, showing meandering or wavy lines, or a series of nodule-like designs covering the entire blade.

Under the Mughals a truly beautiful weapon was developed, and the design of the sword probably reached its peak during the reign of Jehangir (1605-1627 A.D.). Not only was the Mughal sword a superb cutting instrument, but also one with great aesthetic appeal. This combination of functional efficiency and display value added greatly to the mystique of the sword. In the early years of Mughal rule, the embellishment of the hilt and blade was done so that the practical value of the weapon was not impaired.

Practicality and aesthetics were in balance, so that the sword had the flawless perfection of a work of art. In later times, during Aurangzeb's reign (1658-1707 A.D.), the desire for display overcame the importance of function and the sword became a mere ornament, a personal piece of jewellery. The days of the artist craftsmen were numbered. The decorative designs became more crowded and simply filled every inch of space. Even blades were lavishly chiselled in relief with animal or human figures, thus damaging the surface and such blades become useless as weapons.

The Mughals established workshops *(karkhanas)* for the making of swords and some of the most exquisite items still in existence come from this period. But the tradition was also widespread across the countryside and certain small towns villages and boasted concentration of men of the *lohar* (iron smith) caste who worked as confederations of producers and sold their weapons in local or regional markets. In some areas, such as Rohilkhand in the north and in Rajasthan, the skills of sword making and swordsmanship are preserved to this day.

THE RAJPUTS, MARATHAS AND THE NEPALESE

The Mughals maintained a friendly alliance with the powerful kingdoms of Rajasthan, by which the Rajputs were allowed complete internal autonomy in return for accepting the great Mughal as their emperor. This arrangement ensured peace and worked satisfactorily. After the death of Aurangzeb in 1707 A.D., the Rajputs regained their independence. They were later incorporated into the Maratha empire.

Abdul Aziz in his *Arms and Jewellery of the Indian Mughals* mentions that the traditional Rajput *khanda* remained an important weapon during Mughal times. It had changed over the years and now had a broad straight blade,

widening slightly towards the point. The blade is generally ninety centimetres in length. It is single-edged from the top and double edged towards the point. Most *khandas* of the seventeenth and eighteenth centuries, found chiefly in museums, have blades reinforced with narrow fretted strips of steel running down the length of the reverse edge and several inches down the edge from the root, enabling the blade to be light and elastic while the reinforcement gave it strength and stiffness. The old Indian hilt was supplanted and improved by the Hindu basket hilt, which was padded to reduce the shock of blows. The basket hilt may have been derived from similarly hilted European swords. From the top of the pommel protruded a spike which not only acted as a guard for the arm but could also be gripped by the left hand while making a two handed stroke. This increased the impact of the blow and in many respects the *khanda* was the most effective, versatile long-bladed weapon ever developed. The *khanda* was a cutting and slashing weapon. The sword that James Tod mentions as being worshipped was the *khanda*, probably mounted by the old Indian hilt. He goes on to add that tradition has hallowed the two edged

TALWAR, RAJPUT (UDAIPUR), 18TH CENTURY A.D., NATIONAL MUSEUM.
This talwar has a standard Indian hilt with guard, and the blade is delicately engraved with figures of Hindu gods and goddesses, and embellished with gold. Devnagri (Hindi) script adorns the area near the root of the blade.

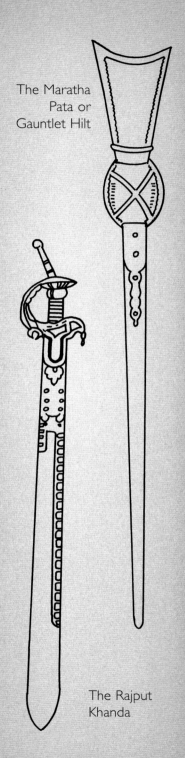

The Maratha Pata or Gauntlet Hilt

The Rajput Khanda

khanda of Mewar, investing it with a mysterious origin. It is supposed to be the enchanted weapon fabricated by Viswacarma with which he girded the founder of the race and led him forth to the conquest of Chittor.

The *talwar* with the Indian hilt and the *khanda* with the basket hilt may be considered the national swords of India.

Another sword which deserves mention is the *sirohi* or serye. The name is derived from an erstwhile princely state in Rajasthan. Egerton says that the chief favourite of all the various swords found throughout Rajputana is the *sirohi*, a slightly curved blade, shaped like that of Damascus. In Sirohi town, swords are still made and most have watered steel blades.

A sword popular with the Rajputs and Marathas was one with a hilt big enough to be used with both hands. These hilts, necessarily, were long and had short quillons. The blades of these weapons were very broad, heavy and single edged. They were wielded more like battle axes and could deliver a shattering blow.

The armourers of the Rajputs, the Gadi Lohars, are today a wandering tribe of nomads. Their home was originally Chittor, where being experts at getting the right combination of heat, metal and forging, they produced top quality weapons and armour for their masters. After the fall of Chittor to Akbar in 1567, they left Chittor swearing never to return until the citadel was freed and the enemy banished. They have wandered for 400 years in their decorated black bullock carts, earning their living making agricultural implements and tools instead of swords and spears. In the early 1950s, Prime Minister Nehru personally led them back to a free Chittor but, their nomadic habits ingrained for centuries, Gadi Lohars wander still.

The rise of Maratha power during the second half of the seventeenth century introduced a new factor in Indian politics. For the first time, the Marathas organized themselves into a national state and Shivaji was the catalyst for their unity. At the time of his death, Shivaji left an extensive kingdom including a wide swathe of the present Maharashtra, and large tracts of Karnataka and Tamil Nadu including Tanjore. The Maratha nation that he built up defied the Mughal Empire during and after Aurangzeb, and remained a dominant power in India during the eighteenth century. They even planted their flag on the border of Afghanistan in 1758. The Marathas also competed with the

War—Almost A Sport

For the Rajputs, war was a way of life and therefore weapons were important. An incident taken from the manuscript of the Chief of Sadri by Tod is richly illustrative of this. In the 1490s Rana Kombha's brother Soorajmal rebelled. The Rana sent his son Prithi Raj to put down the rebellion. The battle between nephew and uncle was fierce and many fell on both sides; worn out they mutually retired from the field and camped in sight of each other.

That evening Prithi Raj visited his wounded uncle, whom he found in a small tent. Soorajmal rose from his pallet and met his nephew with customary respect, as if nothing unusual had occurred, and the following dialogue ensued.

Prithi Raj:' Well Uncle, how are your wounds?'
Soorajmal: 'Quite healed, my child, since I have the pleasure of seeing you.'
Prithi Raj,:' But uncle although I have not yet seen my father, I first ran to see you, and I am very hungry; have you anything to eat?'
Dinner was soon served and the extraordinary pair sat down and ate off the same platter.
Prithi Raj:'You and I will end our battle in the morning, Uncle.'
Soorajmal: 'Very well, child; come early.'

In the battle the next day, Prithi Raj triumphed.

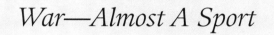

British for supremacy in India, but unfortunately the four Maratha chiefs fought the foreign enemy separately, never together, with the last Maratha war being fought as late as 1818. The Duke of Wellington was once asked which was his hardest-fought battle. He did not say Waterloo but replied 'Assaye', where he faced the Marathas.

One Maratha sword which was very popular not only with the Marathas but also in the Bijapur and Ahmednagar Sultanates was the *dhup*. It has a long, straight and broad blade. The hilt is a padded basket hilt. The use of internal padding in the hilt, an innovation from the Deccan, not only helped grip the sword better but also reduced the shock of blows.

The *dhup* is also called a *sukhela* and if the blade was of foreign origin the term *firangi* was added to it. It generally had a foreign blade imported from Spain, Italy or Germany. English blades were not in favour with the Marathas and their famous naval commander, Angrey is quoted as saying that English blades were only fit to cut butter. These European blades were imported mainly in the seventeenth century, in the early years of Maratha military expansion, when the iron and steel produced in the Deccan was not upto the required standard.

Another interesting and unusual sword developed by the Marathas was the *pata*. It has a gauntlet hilt and a long, double-edged and flexible blade. The gauntlet hilt is unique amongst swords and requires some explanation. The gauntlet covers the arm almost upto the elbow. A thin steel strap at the upper end of the gauntlet anchors it to the forearm. The steel hilt continues below the wrist and encloses the hand. The sword is gripped by a cross bar inside the hilt like a fist, so that the sword becomes an extension of the forearm. The blade of the *pata* is attached to the gauntlet by a pair of seatings which run down the faces of the blade, to which it is riveted.

The hilt is padded so that the hand fits comfortably inside it. In fact the *pata* is impossible to use without the padded hilt. Since it is difficult to wield, the *pata* is only for expert swordsmen. The wrist cannot come into play and the sword is wielded directly by the strong muscles of the fore- and upper arm. The stroke can be delivered in any direction, at any angle, and the force of the blow is considerable.

At the same time the *pata* is well-suited for the use of horsemen. As the blade is virtually an extension of the forearm, it is used for slashing at the foe on either side of the rider. The flexibility of the blade is an added advantage, because if it hits across a hard or resistant object, it merely bends over and thus prevents the rider from being unhorsed. The length of the blade, which can be from a hundred and twenty to a hundred and fifty centimetres, also suits such use.

It has been suggested that the *pata* is a development of the Rajput *katar (jamdhar)* which also has a transverse grip. The side bars extend to the forearm and some *katars* have a hand guard, which makes a short gauntlet.

Egerton, quoting from Capt. Mundys journal, recounts a demonstration of the *pata*:

The gauntlet sword, whose blade is a full five feet long, in the hands of a practiced swordsman appears a terrible weapon, though to those unaccustomed to its use, it is but an awkward instrument. After a display of sundry sweeping and rotary cuts that would have severed a bull's neck, four small limes were placed on the ground, equidistant round the circle and the performer describing a variety of revolutions not unlike an exaggerated waltz, approached them alternately and without pausing in his giddy career, divided each of them in two with a well aimed horizontal cut.

That was in 1827 A.D. I have seen a similar performance at Ujjain in recent years.

While the better Maratha swords were decorated with *koftgari* work and others were chiselled in relief, it can be said that the Marathas were not unduly concerned with such refinements. A sword had to be well-made, but aesthetics had low priority.

In 879 A.D. Nepal threw off the Tibetan yoke and began its journey as an independent state. For the next few centuries however, little is known of the history of Nepal. From the eleventh

❖ SACRIFICIAL SWORD, RAJPUT, LATE 17TH CENTURY A.D., NATIONAL MUSEUM. *The broad blade is engraved with figures of gods and goddesses, and its back edge is reinforced like the letter 'T' in section. The sword was used to sacrifice buffaloes during the festival of Dussehra.*

to the fourteenth centuries a loose sovereignty was exercised by the Indian princes of Mithila in Bihar. In 1324 A.D. a Rajput ruler, Harisimha, invaded Nepal and established himself as king, though he left undisturbed the various local princes who accepted his suzerainty. Harishimha's descendants continued to rule till, in 1426 A.D., power was unwisely divided by a partition of inheritance, and there arose the two rival principalities of Kathmandu and Bhatgaon. The quarrels between them led to the conquest of the country, in 1768 A.D., by the Gurkhas, a tribe from the western Himalayas. However, despite the Gurkha invasion, the ruling Rajput families maintained their position and continue to do so till the present day.

The Gurkhas, a tough, warlike race, are of mixed Mongolian and Rajput stock, with the characteristics of the former predominating. The Rajputs established the Hindu religion in the region, though the Newars of Nepal are Buddhists. Never having come under Muslim rule, Nepal is often compared to India during medieval times, before the advent of the Muslims.

The Gurkhas built up a powerful state and being checked in the north by the Chinese, advanced south extending their dominion from the river Tista in the east to the Sutlej in the west, thus holding the country on the northern frontier of Hindustan. Their expansion resulted in war in 1814 A.D. with the British, who initially suffered several reverses, and it was only after two years of war that the Nepalese ceded the districts of Garhwal and Kumaon in the west and Sikkim in the east.

The two sword forms associated with Nepal are the *kukri* and the *kora*. The *kukri* has a short, heavy, forward angled blade which broadens towards the tip. The length of the blade is only about thirty-five to forty centimetres but it is heavier towards the point, which adds to the effectiveness of the blow.

The root of the edge of a *kukri* blade has a semicircular nick about one and a half centimetre deep and a projecting tooth at the bottom. This, supposedly, represents the female generative organ and is intended to make the blade more effective. The hilt is straight and without a guard. It is made of metal, horn or ivory and sometimes has carved foliate embellishments in deep relief.

The *kukri* is the national weapon of Nepal but its form suggests Indian ancestry. The kopis blade is similar to swords depicted at Ajanta as well as the Rajput *sosun patta*.

The sheaths of *kukris* are also decorated with big chapes and lockets of gold and silver worked in epousse or filligree. A smaller sheath is affixed to the back of the larger sheath in which two smaller *kukri* shaped implements are housed—a blunt sharpening steel and a small skinning knife.

The *kukri* is also used as an implement for cutting through the thick jungles of the Terai and the Himalayan slopes. It has therefore always retained its functional and utilitarian character.

It is maintained that a Gurkha never sheaths his *kukri* without first drawing blood with it, and most Gurkhas still swear by this custom even today.

The *kora* is the historical war weapon of the Gurkhas and has been in use for centuries. The blade, though longer than that of a *kukhri*, is short, only measuring about sixty

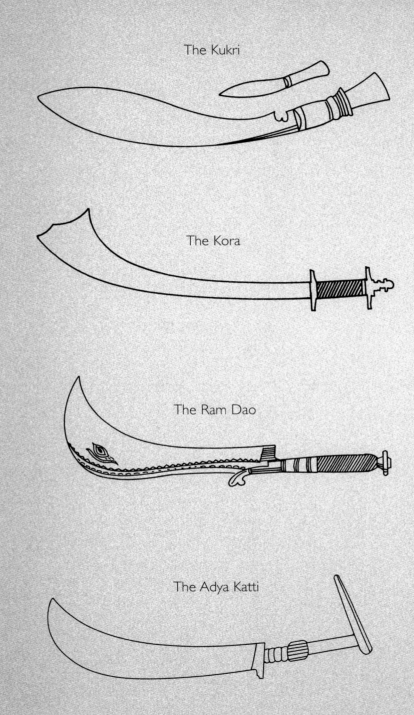

The Kukri

The Kora

The Ram Dao

The Adya Katti

Maratha Warfare

The Maratha system of warfare, so successful in the seventeenth and early eighteenth centuries, deserves a mention. It was Shivaji's genius that laid the foundations of the Maratha military reputation. The heavy Mughal cavalry, fully protected by armour, and the large force of elephants with their towers full of armed men, were able to manoeuvre fairly easily in battles fought on the north and central Indian plains. But on the rugged and hilly Deccan country, the shortcomings of the Mughal army were clearly visible against the lightly equipped and more mobile cavalry of the Marathas, who manoeuvred with lightning rapidity.

The cavalry consisted of two classes of men: the *silladars,* or gentlemen, who provided a horse at their own expense, and the *bargirs* who were supplied with a horse by the state. The cavalry was equipped with spear, sword and shield, with a proportion of them also carrying matchlocks. Their dress consisted of tight breeches, a quilted coat, a sash round the waist which was used to gird on the sword, and a turban which was fastened by passing a fold of it under the chin. The *bhagwa jhanda* or swallow tailed, deep-orange flag became their symbol.

Characterized by their extreme mobility, 50,000 to 60,000 Maratha horses could advance across the country for many days in succession, covering more than 50 miles per day. There were normally three horses to every two men, which contributed to their speed, and as they lived off the land they were not encumbered by baggage or tents. Sir J.N. Sarkar points out that the efficiency of the Maratha system lay in their vast hordes of horsemen, who could march long distances with extreme speed and secrecy, disperse to forage or bewilder their enemy, and yet combine to strike a blow. Their mobility also enabled them to break off engagement at any time they chose and vanish to a safe distance without giving their enemy a chance of crushing them by pursuit. Discipline was strict and death was the penalty for disobedience. No women were allowed in camps—unprecedented in that age in Asia and Europe.

Around this time, Indian generals at war were often portrayed taking their ease, attired in brocades and muslins, with servants fanning them. In contrast, Baji Rao I, the great conquering Peshwa who invaded north India in the early eighteenth century, is shown in one portrait on horse back, dressed like a common trouper and rubbing some dry peas in the palm of his hand to chew. That was the supreme Maratha general in camp.

Another characteristic of Maratha warfare was that they always used enveloping tactics intended to harass their enemy and cut off his supplies. They would not offer a stand-up fight or go forth to a pitched battle in reply to a formal challenge, as was the Rajput practice.

The Pindaris, pure looters and plunderers, formed a regular appendage to the Maratha armies. They were all mounted men and relieved the regular cavalry of many tasks like reconnoitering, creating diversions and the pursuit and plunder of a defeated enemy.

As long as the armament was simple and the country fertile, Maratha tactics succeeded admirably. Against walled cities or camps guarded by artillery they were ineffective. However, firearms could not be fitted into the Maratha system of war and as firepower began to dominate the Indian battlefields towards the end of the eighteenth century, the old light foray tactics became out of date.

centimetres. It is single edged, narrow at the root, curving sharply forward and widening abruptly to about nine to twelve

❖ (Left) **NAGAN OR SERPENTINE SWORD, PAHARI, 17TH CENTURY A.D., NATIONAL MUSEUM.** *The nagan does not have a sheath.*

❖ (Centre) **PAHARI SWORD, HIMACHAL OR UTTAR PRADESH, 16TH CENTURY A.D., NATIONAL MUSEUM.** *The serrated blade broadens and bifurcates near the tip.*

❖ (Right) **KUKRI, NEPAL, EARLY 17TH CENTURY A.D., NATIONAL MUSEUM.** *The blade is short, heavy, and forward angled. The hilt is straight and as always without a guard.*

centimetres near the massive tip. The weight is clearly at the tip and imparts great force to a swung blow.

The hilt is always simple, with a straight grip and a circular plate of metal below it to serve as a guard, and another plate of the same size above it as a pommel, above which is a domed cap enclosing the spiked tang.

The sheath may be of two types—

one, a very broad sheath into which the wide tip can be fitted; the second like the blade which, therefore, must be housed from the back of the sheath and buttoned down.

Both *kukris* and *koras* are never over-ornamented. Whatever decoration is applied to either weapon or sheath is of high quality and in the Indian style, done so that it does not interfere with their use. The aesthetic appeal of these two weapons is more in the simple contours of the weapons themselves. At most, *koras* have gilded rims to the guard, pommel plates and lac filled lotus symbols on its blade.

OTHER VARIATIONS OF THE SWORD

The *dao* was used in eastern India by the Nagas and other tribes. The blade is about two feet in length, straight, narrow at the hilt, broad and square at the tip. It is set in a handle of wood or sometimes ivory. *Daos* are carried in wooden cases, one side of which is open, where cane bands keep it in position.

The *ram dao*, a sword distinct from the *dao*, is a sacrificial rather than a combat weapon. It was used in Bengal, Assam and Nepal, and has a broad, heavy, forward-curved blade about two feet in length. The handle is straight and long, so that the sword can be held in both hands for a downward stroke.

The *adya katti* was used in Coorg and Malabar. It has a heavy, single edged blade which is inclined forward. The blade is generally two feet in length and is narrow at the root and broader towards the point. The hilts are without guards and made of ivory, horn or wood.

There are many other types of swords but either these differ only marginally from the predominant varieties discussed here, or did not come into general use. The *halab* sword is close to the *talwar* in shape and size, but the curved blade is slightly hollowed or grooved on either face and the cutting edge is chamfered. The hilt is usually of russet iron and has a knuckle-guard. This sword was popular in Sind as well as with the Sikhs. The Wallace Collection in London has several *halabs* on display. One from Sind, dating to the late eighteenth century, has a hilt decorated with ferns and inlaid in gold *koftgari*. The interior of the knuckle-guard has an inscription in Hindi.

The term *abbasi* is widely but loosely applied to several types of swords. The descriptions of *abbasi* swords in the catalogues of museums also differ considerably. It would appear that good quality swords of Persian design began to be called *abbasi*. Most authorities, however, agree that the sword is close to the *shamsheer* in shape.

Nagan literally means a female serpent, and the blade of this sword is serpentine. The *nagan* does not generally have a sheath. The *sapola* is a sword with a bifurcated point. The *salapa* is a sword with a crutch hilt, which has a small projection sideways to serve as a hand rest, and the *kirich* is a European rapier-type of sword, which came into limited use in India in the eighteenth century.

DAGGERS

The dagger, with its short blade, has always been a thrusting or stabbing weapon, unlike the long bladed sword, which could be designed not only as a thrusting weapon but also as a cutting and slashing weapon. The dagger has generally been an auxiliary weapon for soldiers and was used in close combat. It was also part of the formal attire of courtiers and other civilians.

In the eastern world there has been constant cultural cross fertilization and individual designs have spread far beyond their places of origin. Consequently, there is a vast variety of daggers in India, some designed as combat weapons, others as items of personal adornment, and yet others which are products of pure fantasy.

As the variety in daggers is legion, we will have to restrict ourselves to those that represent the main types of combat weapons. The most interesting and effective Indian dagger is the *katar* or *jamdhar*. Found only in India, it has a hilt which consists of two parallel arms extending backwards from the blade. These are connected by two or more cross pieces which form the grip and are set near the centre of the arms. The blade, always double-edged, is triangular in shape and usually thickens at the point. The total length is generally from one to three feet, half of which is the blade. The Maratha *patta* has a similar construction and has, probably, evolved from the *katar*.

The usual dagger, when held naturally in the hand, is at a right angle to the arm and the force of the forearm drives it home. However the *katar* or

Facing page

❖ JAMBIA, OMANI, E. JAIWANT PAUL COLLECTION. *With a wooden hilt and a curved, double-edged blade, this jambia has a silver sheath with an exaggerated curve extending well beyond the point of the blade.*

jamdhar is held by the cross grip and the blade is in line with the forearm rather than perpendicular to it, so that when it is thrust forward like a straight punch, it has not only the force of the forearm behind it but also the weight of the body, which makes it a redoubtable weapon. Thrust in this manner the blade, which generally has a thickened point, can even split open chain mail. The purpose of thickening the point is to pierce and break the mail rings.

There are several variants of the *katar*. Some have ornamented hand guards, others have double blades, while others have a central blade with opening pivoted arms on each side. *Katar* blades are straight as a rule, but occasionally one can come across one with a curved blade. In the nineteenth century, *katars* were sometimes made with a pair of wheel lock pistols, their barrels attached to the hilt arms with triggers protruding between them.

The decorations on the *katar* can be very imaginative. There is a beautiful *katar* from Jaipur in the Wallace Collection in London, datable to the early nineteenth century and it is described, thus:

The hilt is of the usual form, delicately fashioned and thickly overlaid with plates of gold, enamelled translucent crimson and most profusely decorated with floral shaped settings, encrusted with table and rose diamonds, cabochon rubies and emeralds. The blade is 47 centimetres long, doubly grooved down the centre. The scabbard is of wood having a gold chape, decorated like the hilt.

The *katar* is of Rajput origin but its use was widespread. Rajput and Mughal miniature paintings of the period bear testimony to this fact. The Tanjore Armoury once had a superb collection of *katars,* but since its dismantling in the late nineteenth century these have been dispersed over several museums.

Jambias were originally of Arabic origin but are popular all over West Asia and India. Their distinguishing feature is a curved blade, usually double-edged and often ribbed. Hilts are their easiest identifiable features, ranging from fan shaped pommels to the smaller, flat-topped Indo-Persian style. Though the general shape of the hilt and the blade remains the same in different countries, the sheath can differ considerably. The Omani dagger is basically a *jambia,* but the sheath has an exaggerated curve extending well beyond the point of the blade and curving upwards, giving the sheathed dagger a dramatic and ornate appearance. The Omani dagger is even today an essential part of formal attire in the Sultanate. The hilts of *jambias* are made of wood, horn, ivory, bone and metal. Silver sheet and studs decorate the hilt and the sheath.

Somewhat similar to the *jambias* are the *khanjars*, which have a curved blade of watered steel and a hilt reminiscent of a pistol butt. Though *khanjars* probably originated in Turkey, they became extremely popular in India, where they are apt to be more elaborately decorated than any other type of dagger. The hilts are made of ivory, jade, crystal, agate and are frequently set with precious and semi-precious stones. The sheaths are also studded to match the hilts. In the Wallace Collection is an exquisite *khanjar* from Delhi from the early nineteenth century. It has a pistol-shaped grip of pale green jade inlaid with tendrils of flowers in gold, set with cabochon rubies, emeralds and table diamonds. The blade is thirty centimetres long, of flattened diamond section. The surface is of sham watering. The root of the blade has chiselled ornamentation.

Straight bladed daggers such as the *pesh kabz* have acutely tapering blades, which are ground back under the grip to form a distinct step. Another distinguishing feature is the broad T-rib along the back edge of the blade. Grips are of the sandwich type with layers of bone, horn, elephant ivory and walrus ivory riveted to an extension of the blade. The *pesh kabz* seats very deeply into its scabbard, leaving only the pommel exposed. The tapering slender point is used for

❖ KATAR (JAMDHAR), MUGHAL (AMRITSAR), 1700 A.D., NATIONAL MUSEUM.
This katar, fitted with two flint lock pistols, is damascened in gold.

Facing page

❖ KATAR (JAMDHAR), RAJASTHAN, 18TH CENTURY A.D., VICTORIA & ALBERT MUSEUM, LONDON.
The katar hilt is gripped by the crosspieces. The blade is triangular and thickened at the point, decorated with a floral design.

67

❖ *(Left)* KATAR
(JAMDHAR) & SHEATH,
MUGHAL (RAJASTHAN),
EARLY 18TH CENTURY
A.D., NATIONAL
MUSEUM.
*The sheath of this katar
is of ivory, and the
fittings are decorated with
floral designs. The sheath
also carries small knives.*

❖ *(Right)* KATAR
(JAMDHAR), RAJASTHAN, 18TH
CENTURY A.D.,
NATIONAL MUSEUM.
*Since the katar is
gripped by the
crossbars, the blow is
delivered as a punch,
leading to the name
'punch-dagger'. The
thickened point of this
grooved blade can pierce
chain mail.*

❖ *(Left)* **CHILANUM AND SHEATH, MUGHAL (NORTH INDIA), 18TH CENTURY A.D., NATIONAL MUSEUM.** *The jade hilt of this chilanum is beautifully designed with a forked pommel, topped by a button. Unlike this specimen, chilanums have double curved blades. The sheath has an upper and lower fitting or chape.*

❖ *(Right)* **DAGGER, SOUTH INDIA, 18TH CENTURY A.D., NATIONAL MUSEUM.** *The straight blade is watered, and the hilt is profusely engraved.*

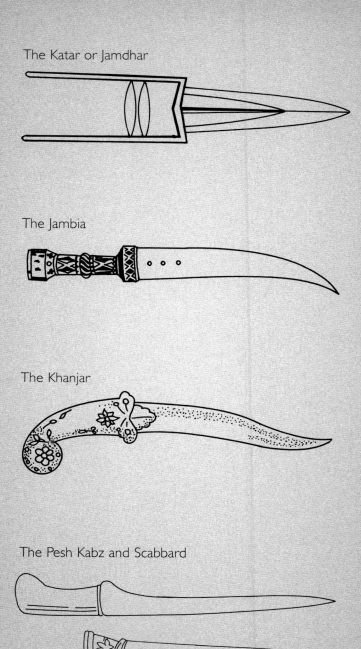

The Katar or Jamdhar

The Jambia

The Khanjar

The Pesh Kabz and Scabbard

piercing the rings of coats of mail and splitting them. It would be hard to find a dagger blade more deadly in construction than this. The great width of its back edge, taken together with its carefully thought-out section renders it of great lightness and absolute rigidity. The *pesh qabz* is of Persian origin and was introduced into India by the Mughals.

The *bichwa* literally means a scorpion. This dagger is originally a Maratha weapon, and has a short, two edged, double curved blade. The hilt, which is padded towards its knuckles, is formed as a loop in which the hand is placed.

The *chilanum* has a double-edged, recurved blade, generally with two or more grooves. The hilt is beautifully designed, with a wide forked pommel topped by a button, and the quillons are of similar shape. Occasionally it has a knuckle guard. The blade is about a foot long and is sometimes decorated with *Ganga-Jamuna,* i.e. gold and silver *koftgari* work. It is not clear whether the origins are Maratha or Nepalese.

The *khanjarli* is a dagger of Hindu origin and is characterized by a double curved or S-shaped blade sharpened on both edges. The blade is generally grooved or fluted, has a mid-rib and a thickened point. A typical feature of the *khanjarli* is a wide mushroom like pommel and a knuckle guard. The hilt is made of two separate pieces of ivory or bone riveted to a flat tang.

The *bhuj* or *katti*, as its name implies, is the dagger from the city of Bhuj in Kutch (Gujarat). However, it was also popular in nearby Sind as well as north India. The bhuj is a dagger with a unique shape. The blade is about four centimetres wide and about twenty centimetres long, with an S-shaped edge. The grip is of steel, circular in section and is about fifty centimetres long, i.e. more than twice as long as the blade. At the base of the blade is a stylized elephant head, so it is sometimes called an elephant dagger. Due to its axe like shape the weapon is sometimes also referred to as an axe knife. The *bhuj* is, in fact, a combination weapon which can be used for thrusting and piercing as well as for slashing and cutting; its long grip is also suitable for two handed use.

The Afghan knife or *churra*, also called the Khyber knife, although used mainly by the Afghans, was widely distributed in India from Mughal times. Indian museums and armouries have this weapon in large numbers. The blade can measure anything from thirty to seventy centimetres and the

The Bichwa

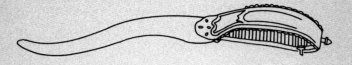

The Chilanum

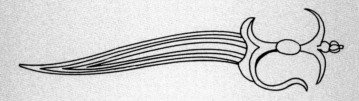

The Bhuj

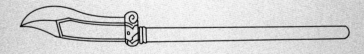

The Afghan Churra

71

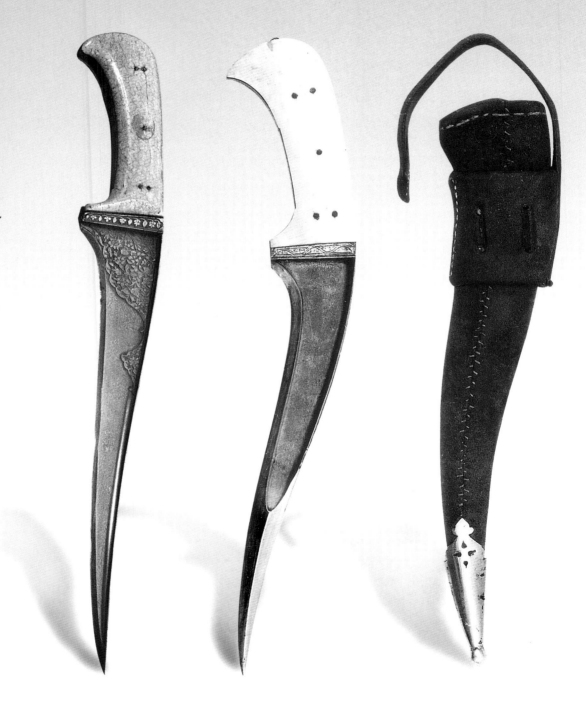

❖ *(Left)* **PESHKABZ, NATIONAL MUSEUM.** *With a sandwich type grip, the curved blade tapers to a slender point.*

❖ *(Right)* **PESHKABZ & SCABBARD, MYSORE, 18TH CENTURY A.D., NATIONAL MUSEUM.** *The hilt plates are ivory, and the watered steel blade is reinforced at the point. The peshkabz sits very deeply in the sheath, leaving only the pommel exposed.*

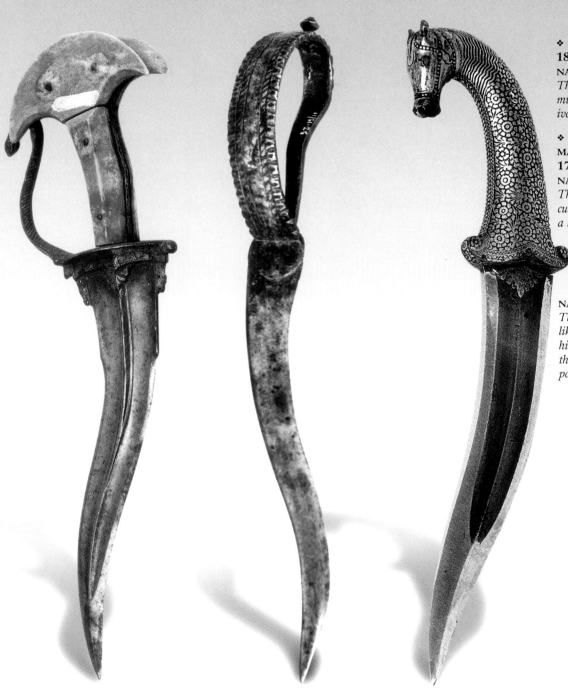

❖ *(Left)* KHANJARLI, **18TH CENTURY A.D., NATIONAL MUSEUM.** *This khanjarli has a mushroom-shaped ivory hilt.*

❖ *(Centre)* BICHWA, **MARATHA, EARLY 17TH CENTURY A.D., NATIONAL MUSEUM.** *The hilt of this double-curved blade is formed as a loop, usually padded.*

❖ *(Right)* KHANJAR, **RAJPUT (NORTH INDIA), 17TH CENTURY A.D., NATIONAL MUSEUM.** *The pommel is shaped like a horse's head. The hilt is damascened, and the blade thickens at the point.*

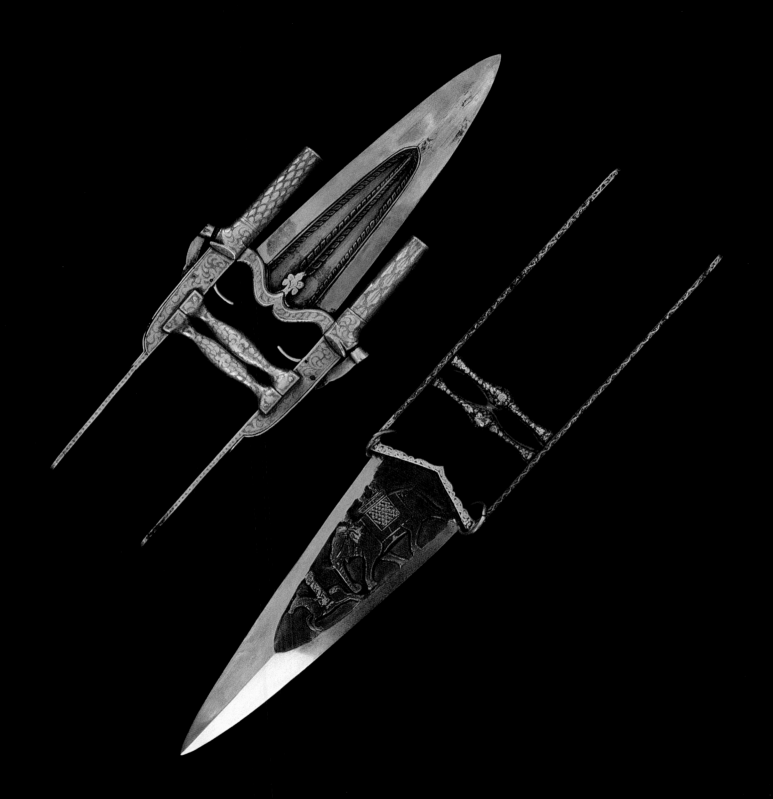

longer Afghan *churra* can really not be included in the category of a dagger. The weapon is single-edged and its characteristic feature is a perfectly straight back blade. The back edge is thick and reinforced to form a T-shaped cross section. The front edge of the blade tapers gradually from the hilt to the point. The hilt is formed by two hafts of wood, horn or bone, or sometimes ivory. The lower part of the hilt generally carries an ornamented metal mount. The sheath is wooden, covered with leather or velvet, and is reinforced with a metal mount at the tip.

The *kard* is basically similar in shape to the Afghan knife, but much smaller in size, with the blade usually measuring 20 centimetres. The *kard* superficially resembles the *pesh qabz*, but while the *kard* blade tapers gradually, the *pesh qabz* blade is wide at the hilt, narrowing acutely and then tapering to a long slender point.

Of the daggers belonging to the realm of fantasy, G.N. Pant mentions a dagger where the hilt opens with a spring and concealed within it is another dagger running into the hollow of the hilt and the blade and this again houses a third smaller dagger concealed in a similar manner. He also mentions a dagger which has a groove in the blade studded with several small rubies, so that when the dagger is raised the rubies glitter like drops of blood. At the Salar Jung Museum at Hyderabad is the hunting dagger of Jahangir, which is studded with diamonds, rubies and emeralds. There is also the personal dagger of Aurangzeb with a jade hilt encrusted with jewels.

❖ DAGGER, MUGHAL, NORTH INDIA, EARLY 18TH CENTURY A.D., NATIONAL MUSEUM. *The jade hilt is studded with precious stones and the sheath fittings are also profusely ornamented.*

Facing page

❖ KATARS (JAMDHARS), RAJASTHAN, 18TH CENTURY A.D., NATIONAL MUSEUM. *The katar on the left is fitted with pistols on the hilt arms. The one on the right is the usual katar with an embellished blade.*

THE BLADE AND THE HILT

THE BLADE

There is much confusion as to what is meant by the Damascus blade. Damascus, the capital of Syria, had the reputation of producing the finest blades. After Timur had captured the city about 1400 A.D., he moved most of the talented swordsmiths and artisans to Samarkand and the importance of Damascus declined. However, it continued to be the centre for distribution of fine weapons produced elsewhere. Much of the trade was with the West, which probably explains the reputation of Damascus blades in that part of the world.

After the decline of Damascus, it was India and Persia that became important for the manufacture of the famed watered blades. The watering effect, or *jauhar*, as it is called in India and Persia, shows a pattern of dark, undulating lines, waves or knot-like nodules on the entire length of the blade, thus revealing a beauty inherent in the structure of the metal. These watered blades came to be highly prized and sought after by swordsmen all over the East. Egerton, quoting from Colonel Yule in his notes on Marco Polo (1254-1324 A.D.), mentions that Hindwani (Indian) steel was of such surpassing value and excellence that a man who possessed an Indian sword or mirror regarded it as he would some precious jewel.

The process by which the *jauhar* or the watered effect was transmitted to the blades was by the old Indian steel preparation method. The furnaces have been described as pits dug in the ground and the fire was kept up by four bellows

Facing page

❖ ORNATE JEWELLED HILT OF A SWORD, RAJASTHAN.

❖ *(Left)* **TALWAR, RAJPUT (JAIPUR), 18TH CENTURY A.D., NATIONAL MUSEUM.** *An enamelled hilt surmounts a slender, curved blade.*

❖ *(Centre)* **SHAMSHEER OF AURANGZEB, MUGHAL, 17TH CENTURY A.D., NATIONAL MUSEUM.** *On the blade are inscriptions from the Quran in relief.*

❖ *(Right)* **KHANDA, RAJPUT, 17TH CENTURY A.D., NATIONAL MUSEUM.** *The spike surmounting the pommel not only protects the arm but can be gripped for a two-handed blow. The hilt is padded.*

❖ (*Left*) **SHAMSHEER, MUGHAL, NORTH INDIA, LATE 16TH CENTURY A.D., NATIONAL MUSEUM.**
Ivory sandwich hilt and narrow deeply curved blade.

❖ (*Centre*) **TALWAR OF MAHARANA HAMIR SINGH, RAJASTHAN, 18TH CENTURY A.D., NATIONAL MUSEUM.**
The disk-like pommel is slightly bigger, the grip is diamond shaped, the quillons are long and slender. It is called the Udaipur (Rajasthan) hilt.

❖ (*Right*) **TALWAR, NATIONAL MUSEUM.**
Talwar with standard hilt and a broad embellished blade.

made of bullock skins, which forced a blast of air into the furnace. Hot, crumbled iron was put into the furnace and heat was applied night and day. Carbon in the form of teak or bamboo charcoal was then mixed with the iron, and the mixture was put through the heating process once again till the iron became partly recarbonized. It was afterwards allowed to cool very slowly, resulting in a crystalline effect in the metal which showed up as watering *(jauhar)* in all its beautiful patterns and combinations of dark and light metal. The method was developed in India, probably about the late sixteenth century and transmitted to Persia soon after, where it was quickly adopted.

An earlier process by which the patterns were transmitted to blades was called pattern welding and was in vogue from the early centuries A.D. Here, strips of high carbon and low carbon steels were welded into one bar which was then hammered, twisted, folded, cut and put through a complex forging process. This produced a strong blade with a patterned surface showing strands or nodules of light and dark metal. This method was also used by Japanese and European swordsmiths.

The varieties and patterns of watering are myriad, but Egerton's classification of four main patterns is most applicable.

Kirk narduban literally means forty steps or rungs of the ladder. The steps are almost equidistant from each other and run across the breadth of the blade. Egerton says that an inscription on one of the blades compares the undulations of the steel to a net stretched across running water. This is the most highly esteemed pattern of watering.

In *qara khorasan*, the wavy pattern runs from the hilt to the tip of the blade, and the blade is almost black in colour. This is next in order of merit.

Qara taban is a large watering design and is a brilliant black against the grey of the steel.

Sham, simple Damascus or Syrian, includes all other varieties and is valued less by the cognoscenti.

The ideal blade of a sword or a dagger has two properties. First, the metal must be extremely hard so as to ensure a really sharp edge. Such extreme hardness is only possible with a high carbon steel. Second, the blade must also be flexible or else it will break easily. This latter property is only possible with a low carbon steel. So in short, the blade requires two mutually exclusive properties. The most common solution to this problem was to use a compromise steel which offered

a reasonable degree of hardness whilst being flexible. The swordsmiths of the time had no scientific equipment and good steel blades were forged by dexterity of hand and sharpness of eye. Failures must have been numerous, but when the swordsmith did succeed in getting the right combination of heat, metal and forging, and produced a high quality piece, there must also have been a touch of magic in it for him.

A number of Persian and Indian blades are incised or inlaid with the signatures of smiths. These signatures are arranged in cartouches near the root of the blade. Unfortunately, in both countries sword makers adopted the practice of inscribing on their products not their own signatures but the signature of some smith who was famous so as to enhance the value of the blade.

One of the most famous swordsmiths of the times was Assadullah of Isfahan who is believed to have worked under the Persian King, Shah Abbas, in the sixteenth century. Blades bearing the signature of Assadullah have great value but one can never be sure whether it is genuine, or a forged signature.

THE HILT

~

The hilts of Indian swords and daggers are generally made entirely of metal. Some hilts, however, have a grip (the portion held by the hand) of ivory, jade or wood.

❖ **INDIAN HILTS**
The basket hilt of the khanda (top), the standard Indian hilt of the talwar (centre), and the Persianized 'pistol' hilt of the shamsheer (bottom).

Facing page

❖ **WATERED BLADE, MUGHAL (DELHI), EARLY 17TH CENTURY A.D., NATIONAL MUSEUM.**
The watered effect on the blade called 'jauhar' has a ladder pattern.

❖ *(Left)* **STANDARD INDIAN HILT, MUGHAL, NORTH INDIA, LATE 17TH CENTURY A.D., NATIONAL MUSEUM.** *The standard Indian hilt of a talwar has a bellied grip that runs down to form short quillons. The pommel is saucer-shaped, and the entire hilt is enriched with gold damascene.*

❖ *(Right)* **STANDARD INDIAN HILT, MUGHAL, LATE 17TH CENTURY A.D., NATIONAL MUSEUM.** *This hilt has minor variations in design and ornamentation from the one on the left.*

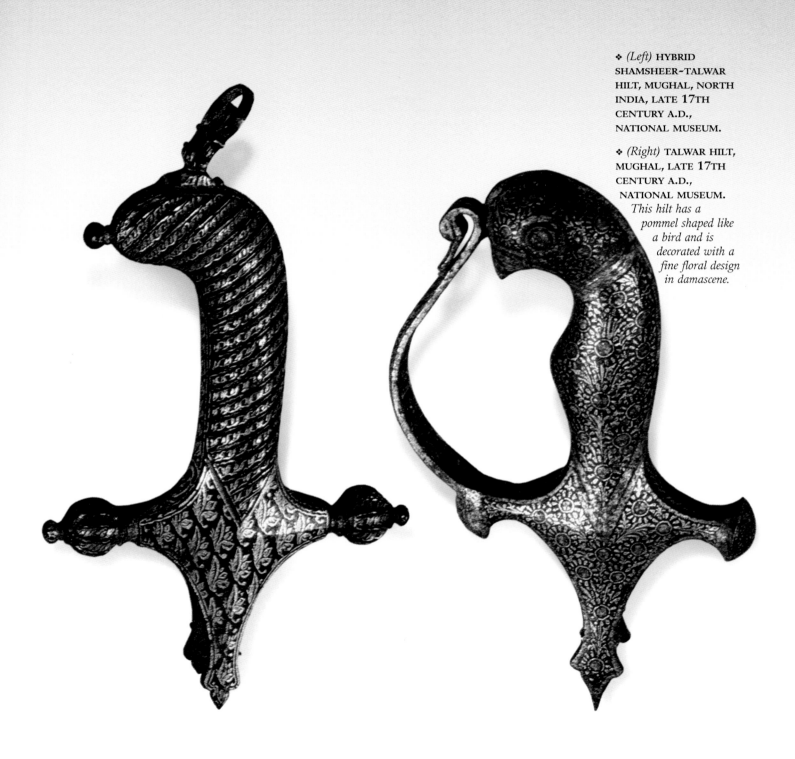

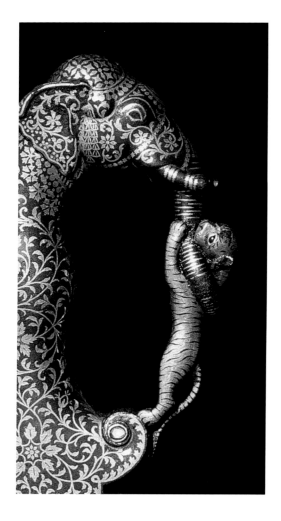

of *josh*, a term difficult to render in English, but which may be translated as a combination of aggression, fervour and recklessness. This may sound odd at first, but when you grip the hilt tightly and hold the weapon aloft, then perhaps you may understand what the swordsmiths mean. The second reason is that men today are bigger than they were a few centuries ago. This is apparent when you view suits of armour in Europe or in India. The average armour displayed in several European museums, would not fit the modern man.

A feature of eastern hilts is that two long langrets project from the hilt, parallel with the blade. These langrets are accommodated in the mouth of the scabbard, which is recessed for this purpose.

There are a vast variety of hilts in India, literally hundreds. However, the differences from region to region are not great. Rawson has described four main types, but I would add the gauntlet hilt of the Maratha *pata* and the cross grip of the Rajput *katar* to his classification.

The old Indian hilt was used throughout medieval India. The grip swells slightly at the centre and it has a duofoil guard from which a pair of

If one grips a sword, the hilt sometimes feels small for the hand and this has often been commented upon. This, in my view, is due to two reasons. The first is the explanation given to me by many swordsmiths, who say that a small hilt that is a tight fit for the hand gives rise to a sense

Classification of Indian Hilts

From left to right:
The Old Indian Hilt
The Rajput Basket Hilt
The Standard Indian Hilt
The Maratha Pata Hilt
The Indo-Persian
Shamsheer Hilt

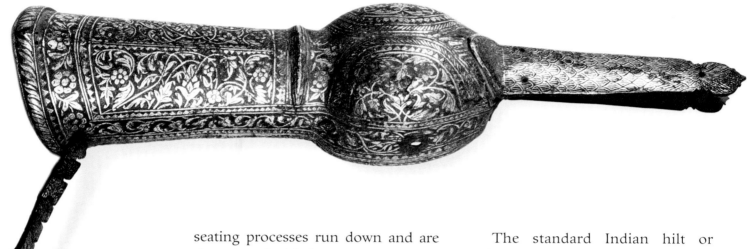

seating processes run down and are riveted to the blade.

The Hindu basket hilt was developed around 1500 A.D. The ears of the old Indian hilt are broadened and a plate knuckle guard is added, which is broad at the base and tapering towards the top, where it is fixed to the pommel. The pommel itself is invariably a deep saucer. A common feature of the hilt is a long, forward-curving spike surmounting the dome of the pommel. This spike could also be gripped by the left hand while making a two-handed blow.

The basket hilt was probably derived from similarly hilted European weapons. Generally, the basket hilt was padded to absorb the shock of the blows.

The standard Indian hilt or Indo-Muslim hilt, as it is sometimes called, was developed out of the old Indian hilt in west India during the late medieval period and was adopted by Mughal swordsmiths. It has a bellied grip which runs down to form short quillons. There may be a narrow knuckle guard, springing from one quillon and curving up to the pommel. The pommel is saucer shaped and surmounted by a button.

The second type is the Persianized hilt, frequently encountered in later Mughal paintings, and of course, there are numerous surviving weapons. The grip is straight and tubular with the pommel projecting to one side. This is sometimes described as pistol shaped. The quillons are long and straight tipped with small bulbs. These hilts never have guards.

Hilts from Jodhpur, Delhi, Lucknow, Punjab, and the Deccan show minor variations. South Indian hilts, particularly from Vijaynagram, while superficially like those of the leading Rajput centres, have some differences in detail relating to the quillons and pommel.

The gauntlet hilt of the Maratha *pata* is unique to India, found in no other country. The sword has been described in detail earlier and suffice it to say that the gauntlet hilt covers the hand, wrist and arm halfway upto the elbow. The sword is held like a fist by a crossbar inside the gauntlet and is welded by swinging the fore and upper arm.

The Rajput *katar* is a short dagger and has also been described earlier. The hilt consists of two parallel bars which are connected by two cross pieces which form the grip. The blow is struck as with a fist and the *katar* is also sometimes described as a punch dagger.

❖ **PATA HILT, MARATHA, LATE 17TH CENTURY A.D., NATIONAL MUSEUM.**
Gripped by the crossbar inside the hilt like a fist, the gauntlet covers the arm almost to the elbow. The blade is attached to the gauntlet by a pair of seatings which run down the faces of the blade.

MACES, SPEARS, BATTLE AXES AND OTHER WEAPONS

MACES

The mace was essentially a weapon to be used against armour, for which purpose it is admirably designed. The spiked mace was particularly effective against the helmet. The *Ain-i-Akbari* (late sixteenth century A.D.) mentions several types of maces and these are described below.

The *gurz* had a spherical head and several pointed spikes were attached to it. The handle was made of steel and was ninety to a hundred and twenty centimetres in length. Some *gurz* were fitted with sword hilts.

The head of the *shashpar* mace had six big ribs or flanges arranged around a central block. The mace head is then surmounted by one strong spike. The flanges present an S-shaped profile and can be aesthetically very pleasing, especially when the shaft and head are damascened.

As the name implies, the *payazi* mace head was heavy and shaped like an onion *(piyaz)*. The surface of the head had uneven projections.

The *kestan* head was a steel sphere and this was attached by a metallic chain to a steel haft or handle. The head was generally ribbed or had flanges. With a straight mace, where the spherical head is directly attached to the handle, the adversary can judge the direction of the blow and take parrying action. But when the mace head is a mobile sphere attached to a chain, it is very difficult to judge the direction or angle of the blow and parrying or evasive action requires much more skill and effort.

The *khar-i-mahi*, the fifth type of

Facing page

❖ BATTLE AXE, RAJPUT (JAIPUR), EARLY 18TH CENTURY A.D., NATIONAL MUSEUM. *The axe head is crescent-shaped, and the embellishment shows Hindu gods.*

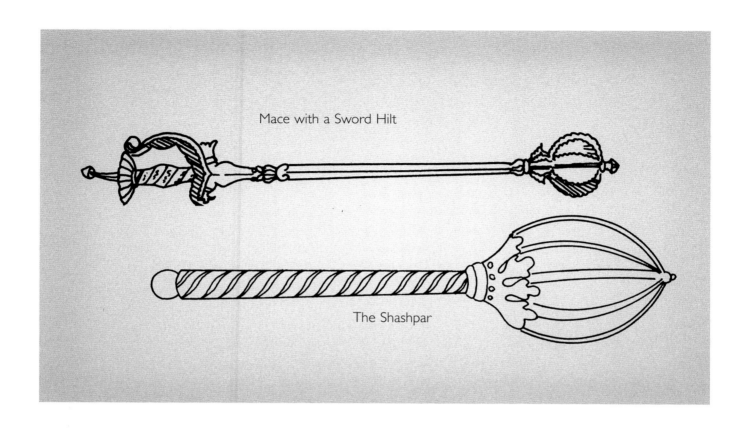

Mace with a Sword Hilt

The Shashpar

mace mentioned in the *Ain-i-Akbari*, was also a spiked mace with a steel haft.

Apart from their use as weapons of war, maces also had a ceremonial role as a symbol of office or command and were carried by mace bearers or *chobdars*. Such maces were made of precious metals and lavishly ornamented. But even otherwise, the handles of most maces were usually enriched with damascening, inlay and other forms of ornamentation.

SPEARS

The original spear was a wooden stake with a sharpened end; as man learnt to use metal, bronze heads were fitted to wooden shafts. On the Indian sub-continent, the earliest excavations of spear heads and javelins made of copper and bronze were at Mohenjodaro (2500 B.C.). The spear was one of the most important weapons of prehistoric

and early historic communities. In contrast to the sword, it was, in early times, the poor man's weapon.

The spear was designed for thrusting rather than lateral cutting. The lighter javelin was for throwing like a dart. The spear was especially favoured by horsemen, and was also used by foot soldiers as a defence against cavalry.

On many of the Indo-Greek, Indo Parthian and Indo-Bactrian coins of the second and first centuries B.C., kings and deities have been depicted on horseback using spears. Kanishka (A.D. 78) and many Gupta monarchs of the fourth and fifth centuries A.D. are similarly depicted. Paintings at Ajanta and miniature paintings of the Mughal school also have numerous representations of the spear and javelin. A popular picture of Maharana Pratap shows him on horseback holding a spear.

Several types of spears have been identified, based on the shape of the spearhead, the length and material used for the shaft, and the design of the reverse end or the butt. Spearheads could be leaf shaped, like arrow heads, or long and slender as on lances. They could be flat or two sided, three sided or quadrilateral, and sharp on each edge. The points could be reinforced and thickened. The spear head could be fixed to the shaft with substantial sockets or a long tang. The shafts could be steel, wood or cane and the length of the shaft varied depending on whether it was a weapon for thrusting, when a long shaft was necessary, or for hurling, when a shorter shaft was more suitable. To enable a strong grip on the haft or the shaft by horsemen, metal rings or knobs were fitted at the centre of the shafts. At the reverse end or the butt of the shaft there could be a metal cap or a decorated knob with a long pointed end, which could be used to shove the spear into the ground so that it stood upright and ready for use whenever required.

Sometimes the spear was fitted with a crossbar or curved lugs behind the spear head and on each side of the socket. These fixed lugs were meant to prevent the weapon from sinking too far into the man or animal attacked, as it would then be difficult to pull back and retrieve. This was also necessary in spears used for hunting wild boar.

Several types of spears have been listed in the *Ain-i-Akbari* and these include the *bhala, neza, barchha, tschehouta, sak, sang, sainthi, selara and ballam*. It is not possible to equate names found in inventories or chronicles with actual surviving weapons. Also, the differences between the various types are often minute, and, as mentioned, depend mainly on the shape of the spearhead and

whether the shaft was made of steel or wood, and whether it was for thrusting or hurling from a distance.

An excellent javelin *(sainthi)* at the Wallace Collection, from the late eighteenth century A.D. and made entirely of steel, has a four sided head with the faces hollowed. The haft or shaft is partly faceted, partly ridged and in part especially fluted. The reverse end is flattened to a feather-like form. The whole is decorated at intervals with floral scroll work in gold overlaying.

BATTLE AXES
~

The battle-axe is also an ancient weapon. Kautilya (320 B.C.), in his description of the king's armoury, enlists a few battle axes. The *parasu* is described as a semi-circular scimitar, the *pattasa* is shaped like a trident and

❖ SPEAR HEAD, SOUTH INDIA, EARLY 18TH CENTURY A.D., NATIONAL MUSEUM. *The spearhead is of iron, embellished with brass.*

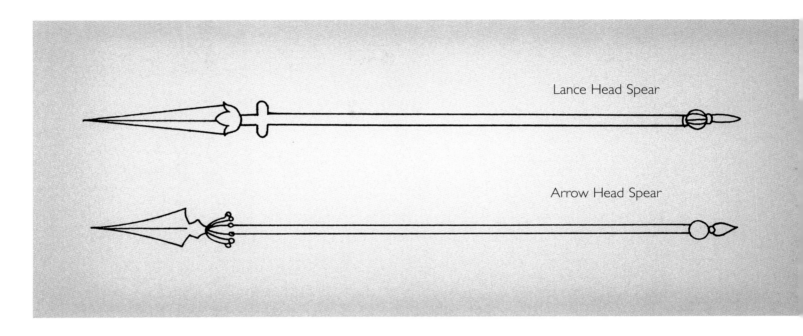

Lance Head Spear

Arrow Head Spear

the others mentioned are the *kuthara* and the *kuddela*. Battle-axes are portrayed in the sculptures of Barhut, Sanchi and Udaigiri, all of which also have important representations of the sword. Battle-axes also appear in the paintings at Ajanta and are listed in the *Ain-i-Akbari*.

Battle-axes do not seem to have been very popular as weapons of war. They came in different sizes, from light weapons usable with one hand, to heavy poll axes requiring both arms. The axe heads varied in shape. Some had a crescent form, others were sharply pointed and yet others were hatchet shaped. The pointed axe-head

was used for piercing a helmet or a coat of mail. Occasionally, the handle of the battle axe had a dagger concealed within it.

According to G.N. Pant, the *tabar* consisted of a triangular blade with one broad cutting edge. Another type was the *zaghnol* (crow's beak) in which the head was pointed and provided with two cutting edges. Sometimes a battle-axe was combined with a *zaghnol* and was called a *tabar-zaghnol*. It was double-headed, the blade broad on one side and pointed on the other. The shaft of the battle-axe generally measured ninety to a hundred and twenty centimetres and the head of the

Facing page

❖ *(Left)* SPEARHEAD, RAJASTHAN, NATIONAL MUSEUM. *Spearhead shaped like an arrow.*

❖ *(Centre)* SPEARHEAD, SOUTH INDIA, EARLY 19TH CENTURY A.D., NATIONAL MUSEUM. *A long slender spearhead as on lances.*

❖ *(Right)* JAVELIN HEAD, MUGHAL, NORTH INDIA, EARLY 18TH CENTURY A.D., NATIONAL MUSEUM. *Leaf-shaped spearhead.*

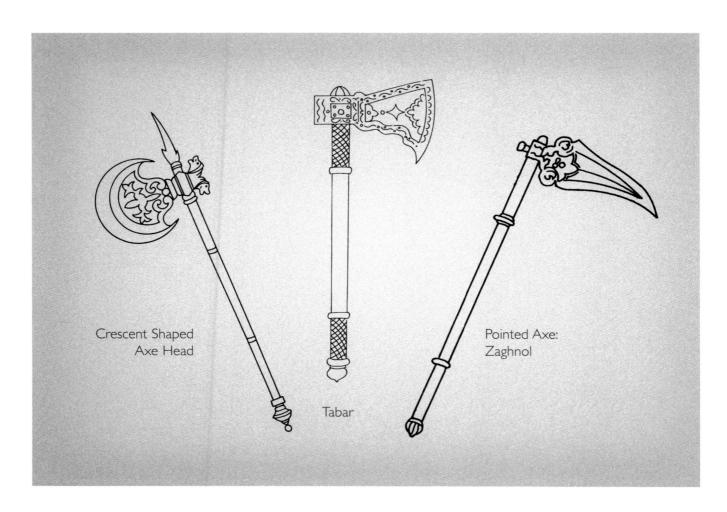

Crescent Shaped
Axe Head

Tabar

Pointed Axe:
Zaghnol

axe five to six inches, measured
vertically. The shafts were beautifully
decorated with gold and silver work.

The battle-axe of Nadir Shah in
the National Museum is a remarkable
specimen. It is inscribed with Quranic
verses and the handle is profusely
decorated with floral designs and gold
and silver work.

OTHER WEAPONS

An interesting and unusual weapon
was the *baghnakh* (tiger claw), made of
several sharpened hooks connected to
a bar. The bar had two rings, which
fitted on the index and little finger of
the hand, like a knuckle duster. The

❖ *(Left)* AXE, RAJPUT, EARLY **18**TH CENTURY A.D., NATIONAL MUSEUM. *A crescent-shaped double-headed axe.*

❖ *(Centre)* ZAGHNOL, RAJASTHAN, **16**TH CENTURY A.D., NATIONAL MUSEUM. *A pointed axe used for piercing helmets or mail coats.*

❖ *(Right)* BATTLE AXE, RAJASTHAN, **17**TH CENTURY A.D., NATIONAL MUSEUM. *This light battle axe is elaborately carved and perforated.*

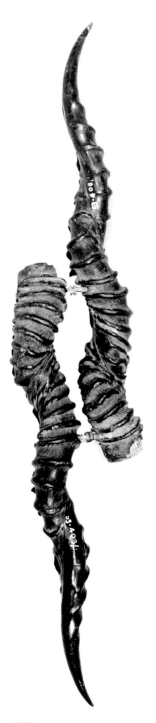

function of this weapon was to tear out the victim's throat or belly in the manner of a tiger. Sometimes a *bichwa* blade was attached to one end of the *baghnakh* so that it could be put to dual use. The *baghnakh* can be concealed by closing one's hand over it. To complete the deception, precious stones can be set on the two rings which fit the fingers which then appear to be real jewelled rings.

Shivaji, the Maratha hero, won his battle against Afzal Khan (a general of the Bijapur Army) by swift use of the *baghnakh*. Setting out on an unarmed meeting with Afzal Khan, Shivaji, suspecting foul play, donned armour beneath his cloak and wore the *baghnakh* on his left hand. As they embraced, Afzal Khan treacherously attempted to thrust a dagger into Shivaji's chest, who was saved by his hidden armour. Shivaji, in turn, ripped out Afzal Khan's belly with the *baghnakh*. In the ensuing confusion Shivaji's troops, lying in ambush, massacred the Bijapur forces, and enjoyed a spectacular victory.

The *maru* is a Maratha thrusting and parrying weapon made up of a pair of antelope horns fixed to a small parrying shield, with the points of the horns in opposite direction. The horns are invariably tipped with pointed steel caps. The small shield acts as a hand guard and is made of metal or leather. The total length of both the horns is roughly ninety centimetres or more. The shield is usually fifteen to twenty-three centimetres in diameter. The weapon found favour with the Marathas and was also used by tribals like the Bhils. The *maru* is found in major collections in India and Britain. The decoration is usually on the steel tips of the horns, which may be damascened and on the shield which is often inlaid with gold or has chiselled borders.

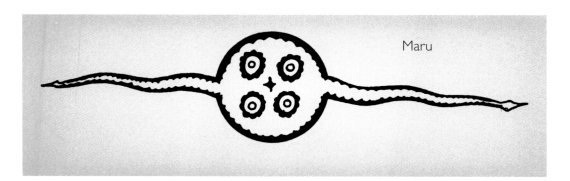

Maru

Yet another unusual weapon which functions as a knife, but does not resemble one, is the *chakra* (war quoit). This is a Sikh weapon in the form of a flat steel ring sharpened on the outside edge, which could be plain or serrated. Sikh warriors are said to have carried as many as six at a time, on top of their high conical turbans or around the arm. In using it, the warrior twirls it swiftly around the fore-finger and, raising his arm over his head, launches it with such deadly aim—according to some accounts, he can be sure of his man at eighty paces. However, there are reportedly other methods of releasing the *chakra*.

Egerton quotes a graphic account, written about 1800 A.D., of the character of the Sikhs as infantry as compared with the other fighting races of India:

> The Rajput and Pathan will fight as Prithee Raee and Jenghiz Khan waged war. They will ride on horses in tumultuous array and they will wield a sword and spear with individual dexterity; but neither of these cavaliers will deign to stand in regular ranks and learn as the Sikhs have learnt, to handle the musquet of the infantry soldier, although the Mohametan has always been a brave and skilful server of heavy cannon.

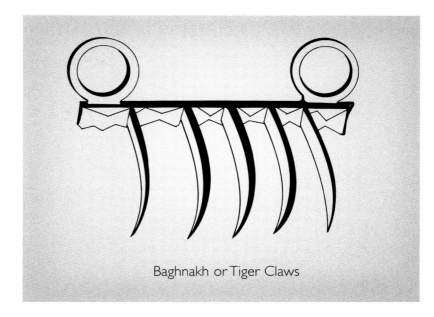

Baghnakh or Tiger Claws

He adds that the early force of the Sikhs was composed of horsemen, who seem intuitively to have adopted the new and formidable match-lock of recent times. The peculiar arms of the contending nations of the last century passed into a proverb and the phrases the Maratha spear, the Afghan sword, the Sikh matchlock and the English cannon are still common repetitions.

Facing page

❖ MARU, MARATHA, **18TH CENTURY A.D.,** NATIONAL MUSEUM. *A thrusting and parrying weapon made up of a pair of antelope horns.*

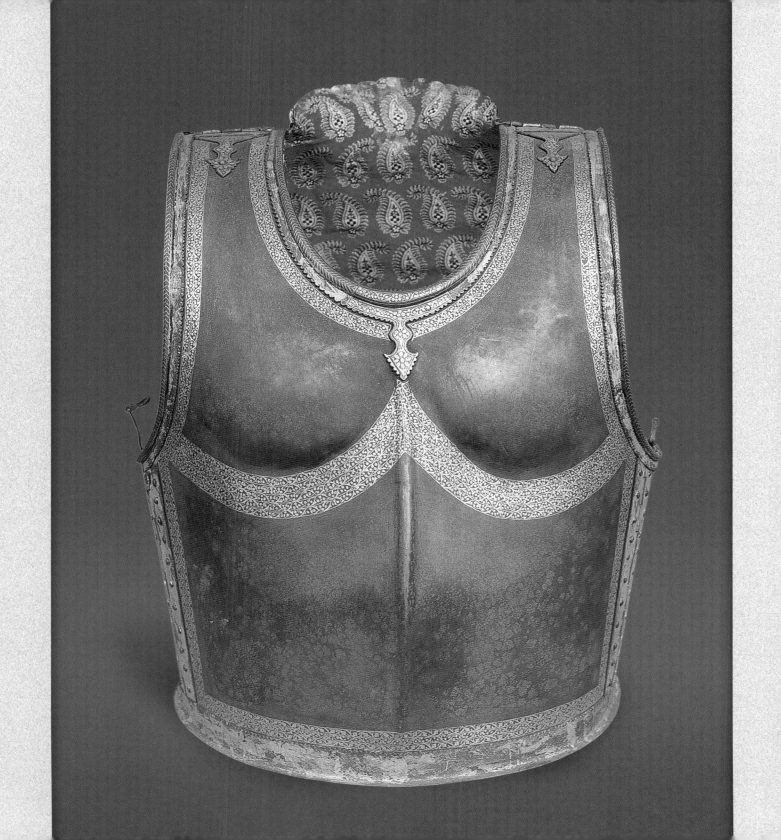

ARMOUR

Armour in India goes back to antiquity, and finds mention in Vedic literature and in the later Puranas (500 B.C.). One of the Vedic chants goes as follows:

> The warrior's look is like
>   a thunderous rain cloud,
> When armed with mail
>   he seeks the lap of battle.
> Be thou victorious with
>   unwounded body; so let
> The thickness of thy mail
>   protect thee ...

Armour is also discussed in Kautilya's *Arthashastra* (320 B.C.). There are references by Greek historians as well, to the armour King Porus wore in the battle against Alexander on the river Sutlej (326 B.C.). Arrain records that it

was shot-proof and remarkable for its strength and the closeness with which it fitted his person, as could afterwards be observed by those who saw him. But he was wounded in the right shoulder where only he was unprotected by mail, that place alone was bare during action, for his coat of mail being excellent both for strength and workmanship as it afterwards appeared, easily secured the rest of his body. Porus' armour was reportedly embellished with gold and silver and it set off his supremely majestic person to great advantage.

Over the centuries armour for the fighting man and his horse improved steadily, to counteract the improvement in weapons and tactics. The improvement in blade-making techniques and more efficient swords, spears, bows and arrows all helped

Facing page

❖ KAVACHA, MUGHAL (NORTH INDIA), EARLY 18TH CENTURY A.D., NATIONAL MUSEUM. *Waist coat of armour for the torso. The back plate and the front one are hinged at the shoulder and pinned on the sides. The armour is damascened and gilded in gold. The insides are padded.*

accelerate the development of armour. Its use survived until the introduction of firearms. Helmets are still used by modern soldiers and body armour has been developed which is bullet-proof, yet sufficiently light and flexible for soldiers to wear in action.

Classical armour too, had to offer protection as well as be flexible and

light, so that it did not hamper movement. All good armour also had to take into account the movement of the body while fighting, riding or walking and the armour had to be constructed so that, while offering protection, these movements could be made with maximum freedom. In the Indian summer, armour could also get uncomfortably hot.

Armour can be classified according to its construction and the type of material used. Some of the more important categories are:

1. Leather and fabric armour, sometimes of several thicknesses.
2. Scale armour, where small overlapping plates, usually metal,

are attached to the outer side of a leather or fabric garment.
3. Brigandine, where the small overlapping plates are attached to the inside of the garment.
4. Lamellar armour, which consists of small overlapping plates held together by laces.
5. Mail armour, made of small interlocking iron or steel rings.

6. Plate armour, where large plates of metal are linked by loosely-closed rivets.
7. Mail and plate armour combined, with plates linked by mail.

Leather armour, made of hide, is probably the oldest of all types. Several layers of hide would be worn and these

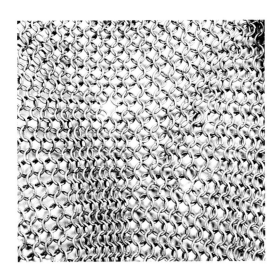

were usually sufficient to deflect a sword cut. This and fabric armour, made of several layers of cloth quilted together, was generally used by the common soldier, who could not be equipped with the more expensive metal armours. Fabric was also used by the wealthy beneath their costly mail or plate armour to reduce chaffing and the shock of blows.

Scale armour consisted of small plates of metal laced on to a foundation of leather or fabric. The plates had holes in them so that they could be laced to the foundation with twists of wire or rivets. The rows of scales overlapped in an imbricated pattern like tiles on a roof, an overlapping pattern that offered better cover and

protection—no gaps were left between the plates. A major problem with scale armour was the lack of flexibility since the scales could not turn on each other—close set with little space between the rows, they did not permit much freedom of movement, which led to the decline of this type of armour.

In brigandine, small metal plates or studs are inserted inside the garment

❖ *(Left)* CHAIN MAIL, RAJASTHAN, **16TH CENTURY A.D.,** NATIONAL MUSEUM. *Chain mail consists of small interlocking rings, each linked to four others.*

❖ *(Right)* PLATE ARMOUR, RAJASTHAN, **17TH CENTURY A.D.,** NATIONAL MUSEUM. *Detail of a char-aina breastplate, with damascene work. The char-aina consists of a breast plate, back plate, and two smaller plates for the sides and buckles to hold them together.*

❖ BAZUBAND, NORTH
INDIA, 17TH CENTURY
A.D., NATIONAL
MUSEUM.
*Arm guards or
bazubands protect the
arm. They usually
terminate in a gauntlet.*

❖ **BAZUBAND, AVADH (UTTAR PRADESH), 19TH CENTURY A.D., NATIONAL MUSEUM.**
The gauntlet at the lower end is made of chain mail. This pair is profusely damascened in gold using a floral pattern with fish.

❖ COAT OF A
THOUSAND NAILS,
RAJPUT (RAJASTHAN),
18TH CENTURY A.D.,
WALLACE COLLECTION,
LONDON.
*The 'Chilta Hazar
Masha' is fabric armour
reinforced with plate
armour. It is elaborately
studded with small gilt-
headed rivets.*

at important or vulnerable points. The plates may also be quilted into the garment. Several sixteenth century Mughal miniature paintings show coats of this type.

Lamellar armour consists of strips made up of hundreds of narrow plates which are riveted vertically upon leather or fabric. Although the metal strips (lamellae) overlap, they still allow more freedom of movement than scale armour. Lamellae, made of raw hide, was light, efficient and above all flexible. Such armour is also cheaper to produce than mail. The Mongols and Chinese used it extensively. Although lamellar armour is illustrated in Mughal miniatures, no actual examples have been found in India.

Mail armour constructed with interlocking steel or iron rings has been the most widely used armour in most parts of the world. The place and date of the origin of mail is unknown. The Romans are known to have used it in the first century B.C. There is also sculptural evidence of its use in Persia in the seventh century A.D. The construction of mail required a knowledge of wire drawing as well as skilled workmen and much labour and time. It was therefore expensive and could be afforded only by select people. Mail was made up of tiny interlocking rings, each ring interlocking four others. The rings could be riveted and the best mail was made thus. Alternatively, the interlocking rings could be butted, where the two ends of the rings were closed firmly but not riveted or secured in any other way. This obviously afforded less protection than the riveted variety. Much mail armour made of iron and steel wire has survived in India, and it is embellished with brass rings around the edges, forming an overall pattern.

The great advantage of mail is that it is flexible and relatively impervious to slashing sword strokes, although a

The Coat of 1000 Nails

thrusting weapon can force the rings apart in spite of their riveted closure. The drawback with mail is that worn along with padded undergarments, it is extremely heavy and a drag on the limbs. However, when on horseback this drawback is partially overcome.

Plate armour, which consisted mainly of large plates, usually of metal, linked by loosely closed rivets and by internal leathers, allowed the wearer greater freedom of movement. As the plates were solid and thicker where they covered vital areas of the body and thinner elsewhere, they offered excellent protection also. Slashing blows against plate were not effective and plate armour also protected against thrusts from spears and other pointed weapons. However, spiked maces and battle-axes could seldom be withstood by the helmet and the head required protection by the shield as well.

Plate and mail armour consisted of plates linked by mail thus combining two types of armour. Sometimes lamellae or small plates were linked with mail. Such combined armours offered protection as well as flexibility without being inordinately heavy, and were consequently much in demand.

In India, as mentioned earlier, armour is of considerable antiquity

and there are references to armour in the prehistoric and early historical periods. E.W. Hopkins, writing in the *Journal of the Royal Asiatic Society*, says that the Vedic soldier (1500 B.C.) carried a *varman*, which covered his shoulders and was either made of metal wire or covered with metal, while for the head he carried a helm of several pieces. Except for the leather strap protecting the left arm from the bowstring, no other defence was worn, unless we accept doubtful reference to some sort of protection for the feet.

The Kushans, a Central Asian people who entered India in the first century A.D., have left behind many sculptural artifacts that throw light on the armour of the time. In *Oriental Armour*, H.R. Robinson observes:

> From the first centuries A.D. we have remarkable sculptures of Gandhara in north west India, where strong Hellenistic or Roman feelings dominated the arts. When represented in their sculptures, warriors wear turbans on their heads, long sleeved tunics and full trousers tucked into ankle boots, such as the ancient Scythians, Persians and Parthians are always represented as wearing. Over the tunic they wear close fitting cuirasses, or armour

comprising breast and back plates, carved with a trellis pattern which at first glance looks like imbricated scale armour. But as true scale armour is also carved on the shoulder and breast of cuirasses, it obviously represents some other from of defense—perhaps quilting.

Apart from Gandhara, there are also sculptural representations of armour at the stupa at Bharhat (second century B.C.), where soldiers are depicted wearing armour apparently made of leather scales. At the Buddhist monument at Sanchi, in Madhya Pradesh (first century A.D.), soldiers are depicted wearing some form of quilted armour. The Nagarjunahkonda sculptures in Andhra (third century A.D.) depict warriors wearing helmets and quilted full sleeved coats. Paintings at Ajanta (fifth and sixth century A.D.) also show warriors in armour. It is clear, therefore, that armour had been in use in India from the remote past and it has developed, both indigenously and as a result of foreign influences, right through the early historical period.

However, from the sixth century till about the twelfth there is little to illustrate the development of armour. It is likely that studded leather and fabric armour was used extensively in

India during this period, with some form of metal armour comprising chest and back plates being used on a limited scale. By about the thirteenth century A.D. one can also assume that the Turks and Mongols must have had a considerable influence on the armour used in India.

However, from the 1500s there is a wealth of information as numerous

Facing page and above
❖ COAT OF A THOUSAND NAILS, RAJPUT (RAJ.), 18TH CENTURY A.D., NATIONAL MUSEUM.
The coat—velvet, elaborately studded with small rivets; for better protection, chest and back plates are fastened to it. The plates are also decorated in gold etched with a floral design.

❖ HELMET, RAJASTHAN,
18TH CENTURY A.D.,
NATIONAL MUSEUM.
*A kuleh-zirah—the
curved steel plates of the
helmet are connected by
mail rings. The long
camail to protect the neck
and shoulders is similarly
made of small plates. The
nasal guard is adjustable,
and the insides of the
helmet are padded.*

❖ **HELMET,
HYDERABAD,
19**TH **CENTURY A.D.,
NATIONAL MUSEUM.**
*The helmet is surmounted
by a plume holder. The
movable nasal guard is
also flanked by plume
holders. The entire dome
and fittings are profusely
decorated in gold creeper
and geometrical designs
in zar-buland. A camail
of chain mail is attached
for the protection of the
neck.*

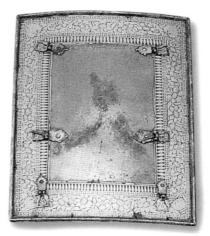

❖ CHAR-AINA, MUGHAL
(NORTH INDIA),
17TH CENTURY A.D.,
NATIONAL MUSEUM.
*The char-aina consists of
a set of four plates, one
each for the chest and the
back, while the two
smaller ones are for the
sides. They were usually
worn over a mail shirt or
directly attached to the
mail. The borders of the
plates shown here are
damascened in gold.*

specimens of armour have survived and are preserved in several museums in India and abroad, as well as in the old Indian princely states. These armours, *zirah bakhtar*, consist mainly of a mail shirt combined with plates and lamellae of iron. Mail armour was widely used and it was worn over a quilted coat. Plates protected the chest and the back. The mail sleeves were full length and skirts divided at the fork reached up to the calves. The legs were also partially encased in mail with the seat and back of the legs bare to ensure a firm seat in the saddle. The shoes were heavy leather *jootis* with curling toes over which mail and plates were attached. Many Mughal miniature paintings also show the *angarkha* or long fabric coat worn over the armour. Helmets were of various types, but the turban, with

an outer mail covering, also provided defence against the sword.

The breast plate, known in Sanskrit as *urastrana*, has been in use in India from pre-historic times, and consisted of a single large plate covering the body from the neck to the waist. It was secured by four straps, generally of leather, which were fastened at the back. The breast plate came in several designs. It could be round, square or shaped like an eight-petalled flower. There were breast plates with floral designs carved in high relief, and ones with a pronounced ridge in the centre so that any edged weapon that hit the plate would slide off owing to the contour of the ridge.

The best known armour in India is the Indo-Persian *char-aina*, literally meaning 'four mirrors'. It included a coat of mail over which four plates were attached. The breast and back plates were large enough to give full protection to the chest and back. The side plates were smaller and cut away so that they fitted the sides under the arms. The plates were slightly curved to fit the contours of the body and were either worn over the mail shirt or were directly attached to the mail. The four plates were joined to each other with leather thongs and were hung from the shoulders by straps.

The *char-aina* plates were usually lavishly embellished in different styles, some being damascened in gold, and others engraved or chiselled with floral or geometric designs. A few were inscribed with verses from the Quran.

Helmets or *topes* were made entirely of mail or mail and plate combined. They could be of various shapes and designs, usually hemispherical or domed, and surmounted by a spike or *kalgi* in which large feathers were placed. Heron or peacock feathers were most favoured, heron being popular with the Sikhs and peacock feathers with the Rajputs. Mughal helmets sometimes carried small flags.

From the front of the helmet descended the sliding nose guard (nasal), which could be adjusted upwards or downwards. The lower part of the nasal was sometimes large enough to protect the lower half of the face. A curtain of mail (camail), long enough to reach the shoulders, was also attached to the back and sides of the helmet to protect the neck and the shoulders. In front of the helmet the camail extended to the sides of the face and covered the brow, thus offering full protection. In some helmets, where

❖ CHAR-AINA, RAJASTHAN (JAIPUR), 18TH CENTURY A.D., NATIONAL MUSEUM.
The four plates of char-aina armour made of Damascus steel are joined with leather thongs and hung from the shoulders by straps. The borders of the plates are damascened in gold with floral, creeper and geometrical designs, while the central field is embossed with flowers in a 'badrum' pattern.

neither visor nor nasal could be used, a semi-transparent veil made of mail (termed the aventail) was attached like a *purdah* (curtain) and this protected the face. To ensure comfort in wearing the helmet there was inside padding of cotton or other fabric.

Some helmets were not hemispherical or round, but oval in form so that they fitted the head

of steel covering the arms up to the elbows. The *dastana* covered the hand and the wrist and could be made of leather or mail and plate. A popular form of *dastana* had the portion covering the knuckles and fingers made of mail to provide flexibility, and the portion covering the rest of the hand and wrist was fitted with several small plates.

better. The Sikhs used oval helmets so that their long hair could hang more easily at the back. Or, if they kept their hair in a bun on top of the head, they wore a helmet with a broad, raised crest.

Armour for other parts of the body included the arm guards or *bajubund* or *bhujaband*. This was a long gauntlet

Indo-Persian armour, therefore, consisted of the helmet *(tope)*, cuirass in four sections *(char-aina)*, mail shirt *(zirah)*, mail trousers, armguard *(bajubund* or *bhujaband)*, gauntlet *(dastana)*, and leather shoes *(jootis)* over which mail and plates were attached.

A very handsome and elegant suit of armour devised by the Rajputs was the *chilta hazar masha* or the coat of a thousand nails—studded fabric armour reinforced with plate armour. H.R. Robinson describes it thus:

The thick coat is made of quilted fabric and velvet. It is long and full and reaches up to the knees but it is split up to the waist. It has detachable scalloped flaps over the shoulders and upper arms. The surface is decorated with nails, or rather rivets, in a scale or diamond pattern, with repeated floral or herringbone design at the borders. In some cases a layer of thin leather was laid beneath the velvet to give a firmer seating to the nails, which were simply bent over at the back. In the centre of the breast and the back are fastened large circular and curved metal plates to protect the chest and the back. In addition to these chest and back plates are smaller horizontal plates above them and one at each side to give more cover. To the centre of the skirt sections, in front of the thighs, are fastened curved plates with pointed top ends and squared bases. The large shoulder flaps, which are separate, are attached by loops and buttons and each flap has a central plate following the outline of the fabric.

All the exposed areas of velvet between and around the plates are studded with nails or rivets in patterns as Robinson described. The equipment was completed with an Indo-Persian helmet *(tope)*, a pair of vambraces *(dastana)* with matching studded velvet hand guards, and a pair of high boots of a matched pattern.

The coat of a thousand nails is not only aesthetic but offers splendid protection. The leather is often lined with *kamkhah* (brocade) and studded with gilt rivets. The steel plates covering vital parts of the body are decorated. Splendid specimens of this armour are preserved in many museums.

The *koftgari* work which generally decorated Indian armour was gold wire hammered into the surface of iron plates in various floral or geometrical designs. Occasionally hunting scenes were depicted. The patterns were limited to the borders and central panels of the plates.

Char-aina plates were also damascened in gold. Scroll work in relief was usually gilded and stood out dramatically against the dark watered steel of the plates. Precious and

Chetak, Rana Pratap's Horse

Perhaps the most famous horse in Indian history is Rana Pratap's gallant steed Chetak. Five years after the fall of Chittor to Akbar, Rana Pratap succeeded to the throne of Mewar in 1572. For a quarter of a century, single handed, without a capital and without resources, Rana Pratap stood against the organized might of Akbar who 'at this time was immeasurably the richest monarch on the face of the earth.'

Lined up against him were also the leading chiefs of Rajputana who had considerable forces at their command themselves. For the most part Pratap fought a guerrilla war against the Mughals, sometimes carrying destruction into Akbar's territory and at other times flying from rock to rock in the Aravalli hills undergoing extreme hardships and 'feeding his family on the fruits of his native hills'. However, before he died in 1597, he had the satisfaction of recovering most of Mewar from the Mughals including all his strongholds, except Chittor and Ajmer.

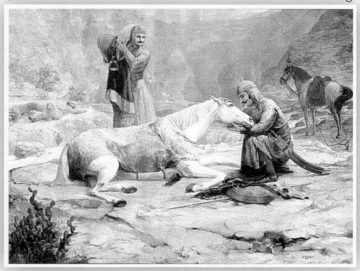

Pratap fought and lost the battle of Haldighat where, interestingly part of his army was formed by the loyal tribals, the Bhils. An incident at the battle involving Pratap and his beloved horse Chetak is worth recounting in the words of the incomparable James Tod. 'In the midst of the battle Rana Pratap made a good passage to where Selim (the future emperor Jehangir) commanded. His guards fell before Pratap and but for the steel plates which defended his howda, the lance of the Rana would have deprived Akbar of his heir. His steed, the gallant Chetak nobly seconded his lord and is represented in all historical drawings of this battle with one foot raised upon the elephant of the Mughal, while his rider has his lance propelled against his foe. The driver of the elephant was slain when the infuriated animal, now without control carried off Selim. On this spot, the carnage was immense: the Mughals eager to defend Selim; the heroes of Mewar to second their prince, who had already received seven wounds. Marked by the royal umbrella, which he would not lay aside, and which collected the might of the enemy against him, Pratap was thrice rescued from amidst the foe, and was at length nearly overwhelmed, when the Jhala chief gave a single instance of fidelity and extricated him with the loss of his own life. Jhala seized upon the insignia of Mewar, and rearing the "golden sun" over his own head, made good his way to an intricate position, drawing after him the brunt of the battle while the prince was forced from the field. With all his vassals, the noble Jhala fell.'

Pratap, unattended, fled on the gallant Chetak, who had borne him through the day and who now saved him by leaping a mountain stream when closely pursued by some Mughal soldiers who were momentarily checked by the stream. But Chetak, like his master, was wounded and his pursuers gained upon Pratap. It was Sukta, Pratap's brother, who saved him by slaying the pursuers. Soon after Chetak fell and as the Rana unbuckled Chetak's armour, the noble steed died. An altar called *Chetak ka Chabutra* was raised and still marks the spot where Chetak died. It is situated near the town of Jarrole. The scene of Chetak's last moments can be seen even today in murals painted on the walls of half the houses of the region.

semi-precious stones were also occasionally set into the armour. These stones were backed with tinsel so that they sparkled and conveyed an impression of richness. However, such decoration on armour was never as extravagant or as brilliant as the decoration on swords or dagger hilts, which in some cases were veritable pieces of jewellery.

On mail armour, bright steel rings would be combined with yellow brass rings—termed *Ganga-Jamuna*, likening it to the meeting of the dark waters of the Jamuna and the lighter waters of the Ganga.

SHIELDS

Shields probably represent the earliest form of defence. The sculptures at Sanchi of the first century A.D., which have some of the earliest sculptural representations of the sword and armour, also feature rectangular shields with curved top ends and broad curved bases. It is surmised that these shields were made of wood faced with leather.

The Kushan sculptures at Gandhara in the north-west of the sub-continent show round shields with convex surfaces. These shields were probably made of buffalo and rhinoceros hide, whose strength and lightness made them the most popular material for shields in subsequent centuries. Shields were also made of hide, turtle-shell and crocodile skin. Other materials used included wood faced with leather, as well as cane and bamboo. The best rawhide shields were made in Hyderabad, Deccan, Sind, Kutch, Bhuj and Udaipur

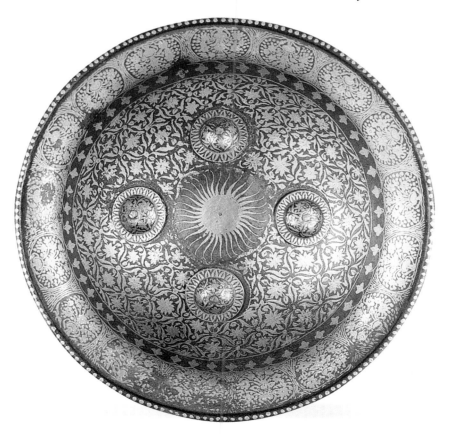

The average Indian hide shield was eighty to ninety centimetres in diameter though smaller shields with a diameter of roughly one foot were also used. Metal shields were also common, though these were smaller in size. Metal shields also tended to have their rims turned over to catch the point of an opponent's weapon.

The four bosses or round metal pieces in front of the shield supported four steel rings on the inner side. Two cross straps or loops were attached to these rings, forming a grip to hold the shield in the left hand. Occasionally, shields were equipped with an arm strap in addition to the double hand loops, secured through two extra bosses spaced a little further apart than the usual four. The inner lining of the shield could be cotton, velvet or brocade.

Though shields tended to be flat, some could also be conical, the degree of convexity increasing as one moved towards the Deccan from the north. The convex surface of the shield caused lance heads or arrows to glance off the curved surface, particularly if the shield was made of metal.

Shields were sometimes perforated so that the warrior could observe his adversary's movements while at the same time taking cover behind his shield which would otherwise have blocked his vision.

In the Tower Armouries in London lies a large Rajput shield made of black hide, that has four percussion pistols concealed in the four bosses. The barrels of the pistols are necessarily stubby, but they could play havoc at close distances.

The decoration of shields, as with all Indian arms and armour, received

❖ SHIELD (DHAL), RAJASTHAN, 17TH CENTURY A.D., NATIONAL MUSEUM. *The outer surface of this convex shield made of rhinoceros hide is lacquered in black and painted in floral designs. The shield is 57 cms in diameter, and the four metal bosses are engraved in gold. The moon on top is the symbol of the Chandravanshi Rajputs, and is different in shape from the Islamic crescent.*

❖ SHIELD (DHAL) OF
MAHARANA SANGRAM
SINGH II OF MEWAR,
RAJASTHAN (UDAIPUR),
1730 A.D., NATIONAL
MUSEUM.
*With a diameter of 62
cms, this rhinoceros hide
shield is lacquered in
black. The gold paintings
along the rim represent
scenes of the Maharana's
palaces and hunting
expeditions. The central
medallion is a sunburst.*

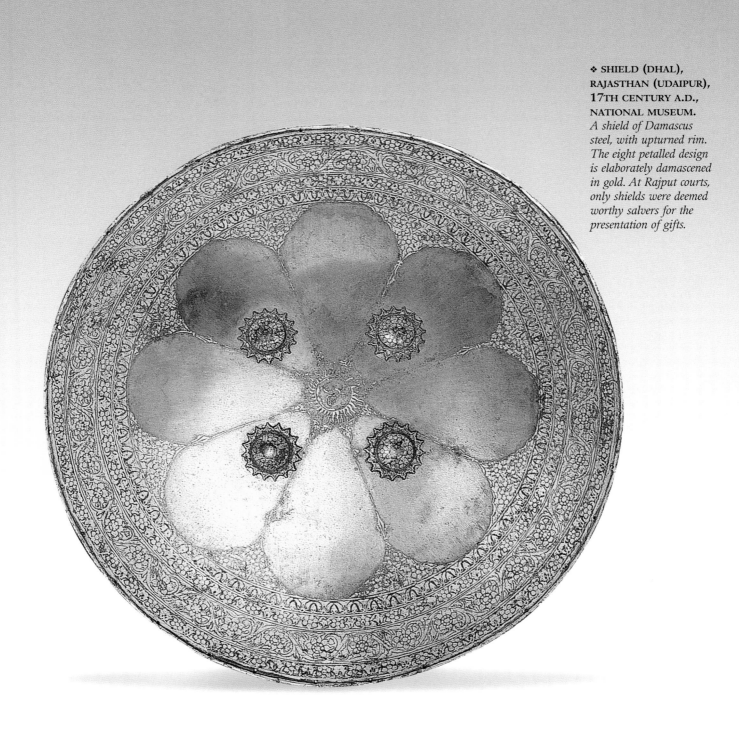

❖ SHIELD (DHAL),
RAJASTHAN (UDAIPUR),
17TH CENTURY A.D.,
NATIONAL MUSEUM.
A shield of Damascus
steel, with upturned rim.
The eight petalled design
is elaborately damascened
in gold. At Rajput courts,
only shields were deemed
worthy salvers for the
presentation of gifts.

❖ HORSE ARMOUR,
RAJASTHAN, EARLY
18TH CENTURY A.D.,
NATIONAL MUSEUM.
A steel plate to protect the horse's face. It has a stuffed inner lining.

much attention. The entire surface of hide shields were covered with floral patterns cut out in flat relief, then lacquered in rich colours with details picked out in gold. The more common shields had enriched borders and a central motif, usually the sun, with the remaining surface left bare. Metal shields of iron or steel were damascened in gold and silver, enamelled, chiselled or lacquered. On other shields the bosses became the focal points of decoration. Shields studded with precious and semi-precious stones were not uncommon.

Like all other arms, shields were venerated and at Rajput courts they were deemed the only suitable salvers for presentation of gifts.

The *Ain-i-Akbari* has an interesting passage on the use of shields by the *shamsherbaz* or swordsmen:

There are several kinds of them, each performing astonishing feats. In fighting they show much swiftness and agility and join courage to skill in stooping down and rising again. Some of them use shields in fighting, others use cudgels. The latter are called *lakrait*. Others again use

no means of defence and fight with one hand only; these are called *yak-hath*. The former class come chiefly from the eastern districts and use somewhat smaller shields, which they call *chirwa*. Those who come from the southern districts make their shields large enough to conceal a horseman. This kind of shield they call *tilwa*. Another class goes by the name *pharaits*. They use a shield not so large as to conceal a man but a gaz (three feet) broad.

Akbar's shield at the Bombay Museum, dated 1593 A.D., is a delicately damascened steel shield, quite unusual because it is decorated with zodiacal signs.

HORSE ARMOUR

Heavy-armed cavalry, shock troops of a bygone era, were maintained by many regional rulers. Not only were horsemen fitted out in armour, armed with bow and arrows, sword, saddle-axe and a light lance—the horses too were often protected.

The horses of the Mughal cavalry were, to use another term, barded, generally with mail and plates or mail combined with several small horizontal plates (lamellae), linked by narrow bands of mail. Such armour covered the side of the neck, breast and the hindquarters of the horse. The horse's head and face was protected by a rigid central face plate with its nose and cheeks covered by pieces of lamellae and mail.

Under the horse-armour was quilted or padded lining. Mail in large pieces, as would be required for a horse, is heavy and drags. The quilted lining, apart from making it more comfortable for the horse, also kept the mail in place and prevented it from slipping off. Keeping mail secure is particularly difficult on the horse's crupper (hindquarters) when the horse is moving fast.

Some Mughal miniatures illustrate a variation of horse-armour made of studded fabric, possibly padded velvet studded with gilt nails. The face and cheek plates were, however, made of iron. There was also provision for a plume on the horse's head.

The *Ain-i-Akbari* lists some of the weapons and armour used during Akbar's time. Under horse armour it includes a *kajem*, a

mailed covering for the back of the horse. The *artak-i-kajem* was the quilt over which the mailed covering was put, which hung low on each side of the horse thus protecting its belly. The head was encased in an iron mask *(kashka)* and the neck in a *gardani* (neck armour).

Horses were an immensely valuable commodity in

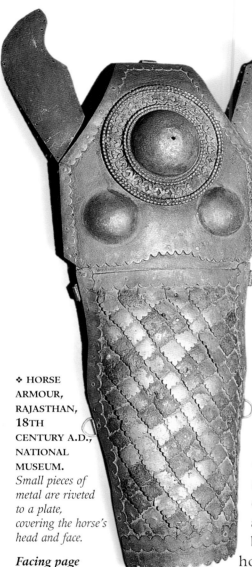

❖ HORSE ARMOUR, RAJASTHAN, 18TH CENTURY A.D., NATIONAL MUSEUM. *Small pieces of metal are riveted to a plate, covering the horse's head and face.*

Facing page

❖ HORSE ARMOUR, CENTRAL INDIA (MADHYA PRADESH), 17TH CENTURY A.D., NATIONAL MUSEUM. *The armour for the horse's face is held together by chains.*

Mughal India, and were one of its most prized imports. The country bred its own varieties in Kutch (Gujarat) and along the river valleys of the Deccan. Many of the finest animals were brought over the Hindu Koh mountains and by sea from Iran, where Arab breeds had long been established. The Mughal rulers, however, also patronized local horse fairs and instituted special breeding programmes within the court and army to ensure the quality of the horse stock.

In the eighteenth century, the Marathas were able to build up their own horse-borne guerrilla armies in the west, by breeding the tough Deccan horses for speed and endurance. These were crucial to the Marathas' success against the imperial forces.

The army of Akbar, as indeed those of the later Mughals, was based on the *mansabdars* or holders of commands. These nobles, both Muslims and Hindus, mustered and provided a specified number of armed horsemen when required. As the *Ain-i-Akbari* states:

> For this cause did His Majesty establish the rank of the Mansabdars from the Dahbashi (Commander of Ten) to the Dah Hazari (Commander of Ten thousand) limiting however, all commands above five thousand to his august sons.

Thus there were thirty-three grades of *mansabdars* in all. They had to maintain not only a contingent of horsemen, but also elephants, other beasts of burden and carts, and were paid unusually generous salaries for the purpose, ranging in those days, from Rs. 60,000 per month for a commander of ten thousand to Rs. 30,000 per month to a commander of five thousand to Rs. 100 per month for a commander of ten.

ELEPHANT ARMOUR

Like horses, elephants were an essential limb of the army in India and were used in two ways, as fighting machines and as a means of transport. Elaborate body armour for elephants could never have been too common. Quite often it is described as made of leather, and the tusks are tipped with sharp metal points. The usual contingent of men riding on an elephant was a *mahout* (driver) and two or three fighting men armed with bows, javelins, and long spears which enabled them to attack the enemy below. H.R. Robinson observes:

> Mughal manuscripts often show the mahout and a single fighting-man in armour. The fighting-man sits astride the elephant's back with a harness around his thighs and a rack of arms in front of him. The elephant armour is shown as of quilted fabric or leather and is rarely painted to represent mail and plates. One elephant in the *Book of Jengiz Khan* is shown wearing a chamfron and complete body armour of elaborate lamellae, but other elephants in the numerous battle scenes are unarmed.

The Tower Armouries in London have on display a rather exceptional piece that includes a steel mask for the elephant's head which extends halfway down the trunk. There are flaps for the ears and circular openings for the eyes. The armour protecting the throat is lamellae, connected with mail. Two large side panels, also of lamellae and mail cover the sides from the front legs to the hind legs. Rings and straps secure the panels over the back. A lining of fabric padded with cotton was used to prevent the armour from chafing the elephant's hide. This armour is reported to weigh over 200 kilograms and is probably datable to the seventeenth century.

Sir J.N. Sarkar, in his *Military History of India*, describes the use of elephants in warfare. In the ancient and middle ages, elephants were used to form columns (*vyuh* in Sanskrit) of troops, serving as pillars at regular intervals, between which the infantry and cavalry were drawn up. In the battle against Alexander on the river Jhelum, the elephants of Porus when seen from a distance presented the appearance of towers, and the infantry resembled a great wall.

During the actual fighting, the elephant provided the commander with a lofty but quickly movable seat, from which he could watch all parts of the field and issue suitable orders as the tide of battle changed. Seated on the tallest elephant, the king or the commander served as a visible source of encouragement to his foot and horse soldiers spread over the battle ground.

This practice continued from the time of Porus' battle with Alexander (326 B.C.) to the middle of the eighteenth century.

Elephants bred for war, with their heads sheathed in brass or steel armour, were used as battering rams, to smash the thick wooden gates of forts, in an age when blasting them with gunpowder was unknown. In Indian battles, whether in ancient times or the Mughal period, the chief use of the elephant was as a rank breaker. The tallest and strongest elephants were trained and goaded to a fury *(mast)* and driven upon the enemy's line of battle, scattering or trampling down their cavalry and infantry.

But the use of the elephant in battle had an insoluble disadvantage as well. The king or his general, seated on the tallest elephant, presented a conspicuous target to the enemy's gunners, or even the cavalry whirling around him on swift horses. If the king was hit or had to dismount from that elephant and take horse, his empty *howda* at once convinced his troops all over the plain that their master was dead and they fled in panic. Or, if the *mahout* was shot off his seat the elephant could become uncontrollable.

At the second battle of Panipat (1556 A.D.) between Hemu and Akbar, the Mughals were saved by a lucky accident, after a hard fight which looked more than likely to go against them, an arrow hit Hemu in the eye, and although it did not immediately kill him, it made him unconscious, and the sight of Hemu slumped in the *howda* of his famous elephant Hawai, was enough to make his army turn tail. At the battle of Jajau (1707 A.D.) Prince Azam Shah and his son Bidar Bakht were shot down on their elephants and their armies dispersed at once in defeat. Many other similar incidents are recorded in history.

129

DECORATION OF WEAPONS

It is not altogether a paradox that weapons which kill and maim are often exceedingly beautiful in form, lavishly and elegantly decorated. Man has a deep emotional attachment to his arms, and a natural corollary to such esteem would be to preserve, beautify and embellish them. But perhaps the idea of decorating weapons goes even further. It is almost as if the weapon, the instrument of death, was artistically formed and refined so that its aesthetic appearance might distract from the idea of annihilation. The thought of death was not banished but perhaps transfigured by the beauty of the weapon. It then became not merely a crude means of destruction but summoned up a loftier ideal. Weapons in India are to this day worshiped at the festival of Dussehra. They are cleansed, greased and even perfumed, for which purpose *dhoop* (incense) is used.

The decoration of weapons dates back to antiquity and there are many literary references to embellishment. In the *Ramayana*, Bharat, when he comes looking for his brother in the forest, recognizes Rama's sword and shield lying outside his hut. The silver sheath and shield are described as ornamented with gold inlay work. Later, in combat Lakshmana tears off his adversary Inderjit's armour, which is also embellished with gold. In the early historical period, there is a reference to the sword hilt of Harsha (600 A.D.), described as thickly studded with pearls. Not only does ornamentation go back to the dim reaches of history; Egerton suggests that even the type and style of

Facing page

❖ TALWAR HILT, RAJPUT, EARLY 18TH CENTURY A.D., BIKANER PALACE MUSEUM.
Hilt is enamelled and studded with gems.

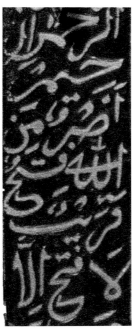

decoration has been handed down from remote antiquity, both in India and Persia.

The custom of giving gifts at the *durbar* (court) of local rulers and at every public reception of a guest, has also contributed to the demand for ornamental arms. At the Mughal court the bestowing of weapons was a mark of high distinction, and a beautiful sword or dagger at the belt of a courtier indicated his position at the court, signalling imperial approval.

Arms have been embellished with geometrical and arabesque designs showing interlaced foliate scrolls. These floral designs included representations of the lily, lotus and rose. Figures of birds were also used for such embellishment, particularly indigenous ones such as the peacock and the parrot. Commonly represented animals were the lion and tiger, which in those days, freely roamed the countryside. Hunting scenes were frequently depicted—a tiger springing on an antelope, pursued by an elephant and other wild animals. War scenes were also popular, showing men on horseback or locked in combat. On weapons owned by Hindus, figures of gods and goddesses and holy verses were often chiselled in relief while on weapons used or owned by Muslims,

talismanic signs or quotations from the Quran were frequent. On some swords, the whole blade was inscribed in relief with Quranic quotations in large letters.

The decorations on south Indian arms, as represented by Tanjore weapons, tended to be more exuberant and fanciful, with representations of fantastic beasts, snakes, fish, lions and demons all richly and deeply carved.

The hilts of swords and daggers were fashioned from all manner of materials, such as gold, silver, copper, crystal, jade, ivory, horn and cut steel. They were all lavishly decorated and often the pommel itself was shaped like the head of a horse, ram or even an elephant. The Bombay Museum even has a separate section for swords and daggers whose hilts have pommels in the shape of various animals.

The large surface of shields provided an ideal space for decoration. The most handsome hide shields were made in Hyderabad in the Deccan, Bhuj in Kutch, and Udaipur—their entire surface was covered with floral patterns cut out in flat relief and lacquered in rich colours; details were picked out in gold. On metal shields, rich gold and silver work was delicately done, sometimes in high relief, with the richness of detail vying with the embroidered work of a Kashmiri Jamawar shawl. Bidri work on some shields shows off the tints of polished steel against the background of a black alloy, the whole effect being that of the finest lace, exquisitely shaded.

Few ornamented weapons from the early historical period have survived, so when we talk of decoration we rely chiefly on weapons from around the 1400s. In the early years of Mughal rule, the embellishment of the hilt and blade was restrained. Functionality and aesthetics received balanced attention. In later times, particularly from the early 1700s, decorative designs not only became over-elaborate and fussy, but tended to cover more of the weapon. Even blades were not spared, and often chiselling or other techniques of ornamentation vastly impaired their strength and rendered them useless. The weapon became more a symbol—an article of personal adornment.

TECHINIQUES OF DECORATION

DAMASCENING

As the name implies, the art of damascening originated in Damascus, and entered India via Iran and Afghanistan. Damascening is the art of inlaying on an iron or steel surface primarily gold, often silver and occasionally copper wire. The pattern is first drawn on the surface of the metal which is to receive the inlay. A channel corresponding to the pattern is then cut into the metal with a graving tool called the *cherma*. The channel in the best work is deep and has undercut sides. The gold or silver is then drawn into a wire and wound on a bobbin. One end of the wire is fastened to the channel by a hammer and the workman

❖ **KHANJAR SHEATH, MUGHAL (NORTH INDIA), EARLY 17TH CENTURY A.D., NATIONAL MUSEUM.** *Minutely embellished with gems, the upper and lower chapes of this khanjar scabbard are also ornamented.*

Facing page

❖ *(Top)* **TALWAR OF TIPU SULTAN (DETAIL), KARNATAKA, 1790 A.D., NATIONAL MUSEUM.** *Detail of the damascened hilt and blade inscribed in gold.*

❖ *(Bottom)* **SHAMSHEER OF AURANGZEB (DETAIL), MUGHAL, 17TH CENTURY A.D., NATIONAL MUSEUM.** *On the blade are inscriptions from the Quran in relief.*

133

❖ SWORD WITH
CORNELIAN HILT,
RAJASTHAN,
18TH CENTURY A.D.,
E. JAIWANT PAUL
COLLECTION.
*The base of the hilt and
the upper fitting of the
sheath are decorated with
gold damascene.*

follows the pattern, bending and curving the wire as often as may be required and hammering it into the channel cut into the receiving metal, until the pattern is complete. The metal surface is then exposed to heat, after which it is polished with an agate rubber or *mohari*, and cleaned with lime juice. Because of the undercutting of the sides of the channel and the hammering, the wire is so securely held by the receiving metal that it becomes a part of it.

There are two varieties of damascening. The first is *teh nishan*, where the pattern is cut in deep furrows two-thirds the diameter of the wires. The soft pure gold or silver wire is pressed into the furrows and hammered down flat, then exposed to heat and finished as described earlier.

The *zar nishan* or *zar buland* type follows the same process, with the exception that the wire is allowed to project above the surface, rather than being flattened, and the inlay is seen in relief. The trick is to hammer the wire down just enough to lodge it in the channel or furrow and then fold in the edges of the undercut channel, which then hold the inlaid wire securely while allowing it to project in relief. It is then exposed to heat and polished as is common to all damascene types. The art of *zar nishan* is very highly valued and is a beautiful form of decoration.

The *Ganga-Jamuna* pattern is one where gold and silver wires are used side by side to give the design a dual effect, reminiscent of the dark waters of one and the translucent waters of the other sacred river.

Another form of damascening, known as *koftgari* and often referred to as false damascene, was also practised. Instead of cutting the furrows in the metal, and then inlaying gold or silver wire, in *koftgari* the part of the weapon to be ornamented is first cross hatched or cut across with sharp lines. The pattern is then engraved with a fine pointed *cherma* on the hatched ground. One end of the gold wire is fixed to the hatched surface with a few taps of the hammer and the pattern is then followed with the wire, bending it backwards and forwards as often as may be required and beating it into the ground, to which it firmly adheres. The metal is then heated and burnished. In true damascene, the amount of gold required is considerable and this makes the process expensive. In *koftgari* the grooves of the design are not as deep and this reduces the quantity of the precious metal required and therefore, the cost. However, if skilfully done, *koftgari* produces an equally good effect, and the ornamentation is durable. There are numerous weapons in various museums ornamented with damascene or *koftgari* work.

Another form of damascene popular with the Sirohi craftsmen of Rajasthan, where good quality swords are made to this day, the surface is first made silvery by a profuse inlaying of silver wire, then gold wires are inlaid to a pattern, creating a lavish and rich effect.

The art of damascene is alive and still practised in towns like Jaipur, Udaipur, Alwar and Sirohi in Rajasthan, Datia in Madhya Pradesh, Trivandrum and Bidar in the south and in Kashmir. Needless to say, except in Sirohi, weapons do not figure in the damascene-ware of today.

ENAMELLING

Enamel decoration *(minakari)* was done on the hilts of swords and daggers and the large surfaces of shields. Less

common was the embellishment of armour and horse trappings with enamel.

Enamel is formed by mixing and melting sand, lead and potash, which forms a soft clear glass, known as flux or frit and is the base to which colour in the form of metallic oxide is added. The final substance is pulverized into a powder. The wet powder is spread on metal and heated in the furnace

❖ BATTLE AXE OF NADIR SHAH (DETAIL), INDO-PERSIAN (DELHI), 1739 A.D., NATIONAL MUSEUM. *The axe head is decorated with gold and silver inscriptions.*

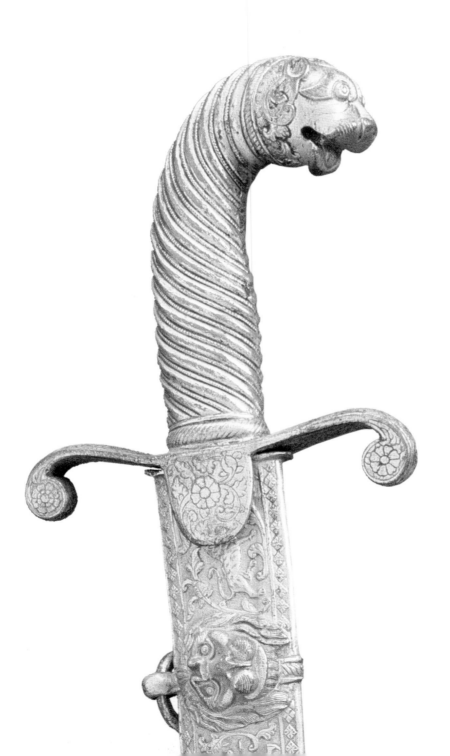

❖ SWORD HILT, KARNATAKA, **1799** A.D., NATIONAL MUSEUM.
The pommel of this hilt projects to one side and is shaped like an animal head. The grip is grooved.

Facing page

❖ *(Top)* TALWAR SCABBARD (DETAIL), RAJASTHAN, **17**TH CENTURY A.D., NATIONAL MUSEUM.
The scabbard is elaborately perforated and embellished.

❖ *(Centre)* BATTLE AXE OF NADIR SHAH (DETAIL), INDO-PERSIAN (DELHI), **1739** A.D., NATIONAL MUSEUM.
The haft of the battle axe is decorated in gold and silver with a floral motif.

❖ *(Bottom)* SHEATH OF SWORD, KARNATAKA, NATIONAL MUSEUM.
The decorated sheath of a sword.

until it fuses and adheres to the metal base. The enamel colour with the highest fusing temperature is applied first followed by one that fuses at the next highest temperature, and the process is repeated. Several colours can be applied in this way but pure ruby red is the most fugitive and it is only the artists of Jaipur in Rajasthan who can bring out its beauties.

The two main processes of enamelling are *cloisonné* and *champleve*. In *cloisonné*, thin strips of metal are bent and curved to follow the outline of a decorative pattern, and then soldered to the surface of the metal object, forming miniature walls that create little cells between them, into which the powdered enamel is laid and fused.

The *champleve* process is the opposite of the *cloisonné* technique—instead of building up on the surface of the metal object, the surface is gouged away, creating troughs and channels separated by thin ridges of metal that form the outline of the design. The troughs are filled with powdered enamel and fused.

Like all other handicrafts in India, the art of enamelling is also handed down from father to son and is the property of a certain caste. The local variations of style in enamelling are distinctive. The enamel of Jaipur is the most famous in India. Other centres of the craft are Lucknow, Delhi, Kashmir, Kangra, Pratapgarh in Rajasthan and Ratlam in Madhya Pradesh. In the latter two centres, a special process of enamel decoration is practised *(theva)*—figures in gold are set on a ground of green or sometimes red and blue glass, while the enamel is hot and soft. The process has always been a closely guarded secret.

BIDRI

~

Bidri was done on hilts, daggers and shields in the erstwhile princely state of Hyderabad. It is the technique of inlaying one or two precious metals onto the surface of a baser metal. This decorative technique, as the name implies, originated in Bidar, a town situated about a hundred and twenty kilometres north-west of Hyderabad.

Bidri was one of the traditional crafts of the region with its origins in antiquity, but was undoubtedly improved and refined after the advent of the Tughlaqs. The craft survives today only in the Bidar and Hyderbad region, but was introduced to Lucknow in the turbulent eighteenth century, as a result of political contact between the Nawabs of Oudh and the Nizam of Hyderabad. Unfortunately, however, it did not survive there for long.

Bidri is the craft of inlaying silver (rarely gold) wire, in grooves etched upon a metallic surface blackened by chemicals. The process brings out silvery designs that stand out conspicuously against a jet black surface producing a dramatic contrast. The manufacture of bidri involves various stages. The alloy is composed of copper and zinc though, in different centres of manufacture, tin or lead is also added. The melted alloy is put into clay moulds and cast into the required shape, which is then refined on a lathe. Next, the craftsman lightly engraves the pattern and cuts it into the surface with a chisel and hammer. The silver wire or leaf used for inlaying is hammered onto the surface. The excellence of the work depends on the depth of the grooves and the amount and thickness of the precious metal put into them. The background alloy is blackened with chemicals and heated, after which the silver is brightly polished. Bidri can also be *teh nishan* as in damascening, when the ornamentation stands flush with the background or *zar nishan* (or *zar buland*) when it stands out in relief.

JEWELLING

~

The setting of precious stones and jewels for the adornment of weapons is no different from the normal methods of making jewellery. A stone

139

is kept in place by claws cut from the metal. Claws may be in various shapes and are bent over the tops of the stones to hold them securely. They must always be strong enough to hold the stone and stand long usage. A second process consists of setting the gem and then gently hammering in a ring of malleable gold or silver into the socket so that the stone is held firmly. A third is simply to fix the stone in the appropriate place with the help of *lac*.

Indian jewellers tend to focus on the brilliant colours of the gems. Emeralds, rubies and diamonds are frequently set in enamel or jade to make floral patterns—the brilliance of the enamel and the whiteness of the jade are used to set off their colours. The way the socket is cut underneath the stone can also enhance the sparkle and such skilful cutting also receives a lot of the jeweller's attention. Coloured foils that complement and enhance the tint of the gem were sometimes positioned under the stone, adding greatly to the splendour of the jewelled weapon.

Some superbly jewelled Indian arms are on display in museums in India and abroad. Displayed at the Baroda Palace Armoury is a sword whose hilt is studded with two hundred and seventy-five diamonds and an emerald. One of the most beautiful jewelled daggers *(katar)* is in the Wallace Collection, London. It has the usual *katar* hilt with two parallel arms and a cross grip. The hilt has been thickly overlaid with plates of gold, enamelled a striking, translucent crimson, profusely decorated and encrusted with rose diamonds, cabochon rubies and emeralds. It is from Jaipur and is datable to the nineteenth century A.D.

NIELLO

A technique known as niello was used for the embellishment of Mughal swords, daggers and scabbards. The polished metal surface is first deeply engraved in floral or other designs and then filled with a black metallic compound, an amalgam made up of silver, copper and lead, heated and poured into the engraved design. The metal object is then rubbed over with borax and heated once again.

When it is cool it is burnished to a bright finish.

gold in leaf or powder form. It is common on Indian weapons and large surfaces are often found resplendent with brilliant gilding.

The first stage in gilding is to beat the gold into leaves which are micro thin. This is largely done by hand, when the gold is subjected to prolonged beating by a wooden mallet. This process can often be seen in jewellers' streets in many Indian towns, accompanied by the distinctive and uninterrupted sound of the falling wooden mallet. The gold leaves are then packed between tissue papers and are ready for the gilder's use. The ground to be gilded must be carefully prepared, being finely cut across or cross hatched with a graver, as in *koftgari,* or being etched with an acid that gives it a broken surface. The gold leaf is rolled on to the prepared surface, heated and burnished; the malleable gold is thus bonded to the roughened surface. Occasionally, leaf gold is powdered and then applied, but this is expensive.

GILDING
~

Gilding is the art of decorating metal or wood with a covering or design of

CHISELLING AND ETCHING
~

Chiselling is accomplished by the skilful use of a hammer and chisel on

❖ HILT, MUGHAL (DELHI), EARLY 17TH CENTURY A.D., NATIONAL MUSEUM. *The hilt is jewelled and set with precious stones.*

the face of the metal. For much of the south Indian work it may have been necessary first to soften the steel of which swords and daggers were made since the relief in which work is executed is very deep.

In north Indian weapons there is often a chiselled panel containing a floral scroll near the root of the blade. In addition, hilts of swords and daggers as well as spear heads and handles of maces and battle axes have been finely chiselled with decorative motifs.

Sometimes etching is substituted for chiselling as a process for making a design in relief on metal. In this technique the design is obtained by eating into the metal with an acid. The part of the surface which is to stand in relief is first covered or stopped with waxes or resins. The metal is then immersed in acid, which bites into the metal excluding the covered areas. It is then washed in fresh water.

❖ (*Left*) TALWAR (DETAIL), RAJPUT (UDAIPUR), 18TH CENTURY A.D., NATIONAL MUSEUM. *Detail of the engraving of the figures of Hindu gods, goddesses and gold embellishment on both sides of the blade.*

LOST WAX PROCESS

~

The lost wax or *cire perdu* process was used to cast some especially decorative hilts of swords and daggers. It involved the creation of a wax model of the hilt and carving in the wax the decoration that was to be used. The wax was encased in clay, with a vent opening from the bottom of the clay mould. The mould was then allowed to dry and when heat was applied to it, the wax melted and ran out of the vent. This left behind a hollow impression of the hilt with the decorative design that had been carved upon it.

When the mould was inverted, molten metal was poured into the vent. After the metal had set the clay mould was broken and the casting taken from it. This method enabled some highly intricate designs to be made.

An exquisite south Indian *bichwa* from the author's collection, is a dagger of Maratha origin. It has a short double curved blade. The hilt is formed as a loop in which the hand is placed. A guard, unusual in a *bichwa*, extends in a semi-circle. The intricate design on the guard could only be the product of the lost wax process. The central motif is the face of a monster complete with tusks, all in deep relief. This is surrounded by a delicate floral design and the whole is surmounted by the protruding head of a second beast with wide open jaws.

143